TWAYNE'S WORLD AUTHORS SERIES

A Survey of the World's Literature

Sylvia E. Bowman, Indiana University

GENERAL EDITOR

SPAIN

Gerald Wade, Vanderbilt University

EDITOR

Francisco de Rojas Zorrilla

(TWAS 64)

TWAYNE'S WORLD AUTHORS SERIES (TWAS)

The purpose of TWAS is to survey the major writers —novelists, dramatists, historians, poets, philosophers, and critics—of the nations of the world. Among the national literatures covered are those of Australia, Canada, China, Eastern Europe, France, Germany, Greece, India, Italy, Japan, Latin America, New Zealand, Poland, Russia, Scandinavia, Spain, and the African nations, as well as Hebrew, Yiddish, and Latin Classical literatures. This survey is complemented by Twayne's United States Authors Series and English Authors Series.

The intent of each volume in these series is to present a critical-analytical study of the works of the writer; to include biographical and historical material that may be necessary for understanding, appreciation, and critical appraisal of the writer; and to present all material in clear, concise English—but not to vitiate the scholarly content of the work by doing so.

Francisco de Rojas Zorrilla

By RAYMOND R. MacCURDY

University of New Mexico

Twayne Publishers, Inc.   ::   New York

To
Karl and Polly Shedd

Preface

The name of Francisco de Rojas Zorrilla means little to students of English literature except those who are mindful of footnotes and have a memory for minutiae. Few of that minority are likely to remember that two of Rojas' plays are the original sources of William D'Avenant's *The Man's the Master* and Sir John Vanbrugh's *The False Friend*. Those English plays are not in everybody's library. Only a few more will remember that Rojas was the young Spanish contemporary of Shakespeare—he was only nine when Shakespeare died—who also wrote a Romeo and Juliet play (*Los bandos de Verona*), a drama based on Antony and Cleopatra (*Los áspides de Cleopatra*), and a tragedy on the rape of Lucrece (*Lucrecia y Tarquino*). Rojas did not know the works of the English master, although he used most of the same sources as Shakespeare did when he dramatized these familiar tales of those who "loved not wisely but too well." Perhaps the significant thing is, however, that these same familiar tales caught the fancy and engaged the talents of two such men, for, as a French critic might say (and probably has said), "By their sources you shall know them."

But few French students worth their *bachot* would fail to remember the name of Rojas, because when French playwrights of the seventeenth century ransacked the Spanish theater for plots, Rojas' plays were among those most pilfered. Jean Rotrou's fine tragedy, *Venceslas*, is based on *No hay ser padre siendo rey* (*A King Cannot Act as a Father*); Paul Scarron's gayest comedy, *Jodolet ou le Maître valet*, is an adaptation of Rojas' *Donde hay agravios no hay celos* (*Dishonor Leaves No Room for Jealousy*); and, most remarkable of all, three French dramatists made independent adaptations in the same year (1655) of Rojas' *Obligados y ofendidos y gorrón de Salamanca* (*Obligated and offended, and the Freeloader of Salamanca*). Add to this the fact that in the early eighteenth century Alain-René Lesage borrowed the plots of three of Rojas' plays for his works in prose, including an important episode in his famous *Gil Blas de Santillane,* and it becomes apparent that the Spaniard's theatrical works were well known beyond the Pyrenees.

It is in Spain itself, however, where Rojas' fortunes have undergone the most puzzling vicissitudes. Most educated Spaniards remember him only as the author of a fine honor drama, *Del rey abajo, ninguno* (*Below the King All Men Are Peers*), which, perhaps, he did not write—at least in its entirety. Others confuse him with Fernando de Rojas, author of the great prose masterpiece, *La Celestina,* which was written more than a century before he was born. But worst of all, some older literary historians accused him of corrupting his friend and collaborator, Pedro Calderón de la Barca, by leading him down the sinful path of Gongorism. The older Calderón, it should be said, was an established dramatist before Rojas began to write, and was quite capable of assimilating the tortured language of Luis de Góngora on his own.

Some critics have also been indiscriminate in their praise of Rojas. A few have held that he was the only true tragedian of the Golden Age. Others have said that he was the most "intense" writer of comedy of his time. No critic, Spanish or foreign, has questioned his great talent or his originality, although many have deplored his misuse of these gifts. In sum, Rojas is now ranked among the top half-dozen dramatists of the Golden Age theater. There is no doubt that his lack of balance (a very real defect of his over-all production) has denied him a higher place.

No general book concerning the life and works of Rojas has ever been printed in English. Even in Spain not a single volume, general in character, has been devoted to Rojas since the publication in 1911 of Emilio Cotarelo y Mori's book, which remains the fundamental source of biographical and bibliographical information on the Toledan dramatist and his theater. A few doctoral dissertations have been written on Rojas, but the only ones which have been published are written in German. Several editions of his plays, some containing important introductory studies, have been published in recent years; and a few monographs aimed at examining particular aspects of his dramaturgy have appeared. Above all, numerous articles devoted to the analysis of single plays, especially *Del rey abajo, ninguno,* have been printed in professional journals during the last decade. But by and large, Rojas continues to be one of the most neglected major figures of seventeenth-century Spanish literature.

The present book has three principal aims: (1) to present essential factual information concerning Rojas' life and works (although nothing significant pertaining to his biography has been discovered since the publication of Cotarelo's book over fifty years ago); (2) to classify his authentic plays; (3) to present résumés of the plots of the plays and brief critical analyses of the principal ones. In view of the fact that the book is addressed primarily to general readers, it includes some background information on the Spanish theater and specifically on the Golden Age *comedia* (for example, the definitions of types of plays) that specialists will find all too familiar. I have thought it wise, however, to arrange the book by types of plays rather than chronologically or topically.

In the discussion of individual plays I have consciously tried to avoid adopting a single critical approach. If one play is chiefly of interest because of its plot—or if it has no significance beyond its plot—little more than a résumé is offered. If another is noteworthy because of its characterization or its technical devices, those matters receive the most attention. In a few cases (which are almost necessarily limited to Rojas' best plays) where structure and theme merit more careful analysis, more space is devoted to these subjects. Students of Spanish drama will perhaps find a few new interpretations of some of the plays, as well as new information on sources, versification, authenticity, and bibliographical matters.

A few chapters of the book draw on material included in my monograph, *Francisco de Rojas Zorrilla and the Tragedy* (Albuquerque, 1958; reprinted, 1966). Chapter 1, "A Biographical Sketch," is substantially the same as the corresponding chapter in the previous study, although it has been slightly revised; and Chapters 3 and 4, "The Tragedies" and "The Honor Dramas," present in reduced form much of the information contained on these plays in the monograph. On referring to the characters in

Rojas' plays, I have used their Spanish names (Progne and Filomena, for example), but when the same characters are discussed for their roles in myth or other literatures, the English forms of the names are used (Procne and Philomela). The English translation of the titles of Rojas' plays is given on the first occurrence of each title, but the titles of learned articles and books, which would not be of interest to those who do not read Spanish, are not translated. In Chapter 2, pages 29-32, there are tables listing Rojas' plays: A. Authentic Plays of Individual Authorship; B. Plays Written in Collaboration; and C. Authentic *autos sacramentales*. In each table the plays are listed alphabetically by their Spanish titles, followed by the English translation. A list of abbreviations used in the book is found at the beginning of the Notes and References on page 141.

It is my pleasure to thank Miss Dolores Sánchez for typing the manuscript and Professor Gerald Wade for his helpful suggestions.

Contents

Chronology

1607 October 4: Rojas is born in Toledo, eldest of the six children of Ensign Francisco Pérez de Rojas and Doña Mariana de Vesga y Zorrilla. Later adopts the second surname of each parent.

1610 Family moves to Madrid where Rojas receives his early education.

1621 Philip III dies and is succeeded by his son Philip IV.

1625 (?) Rojas probably studies at the University of Salamanca, but if so, dates are uncertain.

1630 (?) Becomes active in literary circles in Madrid. Begins writing plays in collaboration with Luis Vélez de Guevara, Antonio Coello, Pedro Calderón de la Barca, and Juan Pérez de Montalván.

1632 In his *For Everyone* (*Para todos*) Montalván praises Rojas for the "ingenious plays he has written," but the titles of such plays are not known.

1633 Performance before the king and queen of *Persiles y Segismunda* (based on Cervantes' novel of the same title), the first definitely dated play of Rojas' individual authorship.

1635 Lope de Vega dies in Madrid. Now established as a court dramatist, Rojas has seven plays performed in the Royal Palace and other royal theaters.

1636 Contributes a sonnet to *Posthumous Fame* (*Fama póstuma*), a memorial volume compiled by Montalván on the death of Lope de Vega.

1637– Acts as "prosecutor" (*fiscal*) in the burlesque literary
1638 academies held at the court.

1638 Rojas is reported killed in a duel but he recovers. Probably composes the comedy *Merry Sport with Fools* (*Entre bobos anda el juego*).

1639 Begins writing a series of sacramental plays.

1640 Publication of *Part I* of Rojas' plays (contains twelve plays). Rojas marries Doña Catalina Yáñez Trillo de Mendoza, by whom he had one son born in 1642.

1643 Nominated for membership in the Order of Santiago but is accused of having Moorish and Jewish blood.

1644 Spanish theaters are closed in mourning because of the queen's death.

1645 Publication of *Part II* of Rojas' plays (also contains twelve plays). Finally granted membership in the Order of Santiago.

1647 Performance of the sacramental play entitled *The Great Courtyard of the Palace* (*El gran patio de palacio*), probably Rojas' last work.

1648 January 23: Dies suddenly in Madrid.

CHAPTER 1

A Biographical Sketch

FRANCISCO de Rojas Zorrilla, eldest of the six children of Ensign Francisco Pérez de Rojas and Doña Mariana de Vesga y Zorrilla, was born in Toledo on October 4, 1607, and baptized in the parish Church of San Salvador on October 27. Contrary to Spanish custom and for reasons still not clear—perhaps because his poet's ear rejected the name of Francisco Pérez Vesga—he later assumed the second surname of each parent. As a child Rojas had little time to immerse himself in the historic atmosphere of the Imperial City, because when he was three years of age, his father abandoned his career in the royal navy and moved his family to Madrid. Perhaps it was just as well. Gossipy neighbors in Toledo later gave out the word that Rojas' ancestors were of Moorish and Jewish blood and that the garments they wore when executed on orders of the Inquisition formerly hung in the Church of Santo Tomé where now hangs El Greco's famous painting, *The Burial of Count Orgaz* (*El entierro del Conde de Orgaz*). But more of this later.

In Madrid where his father entered the service of the Marqués de Loriana as majordomo, Rojas and his family occupied a house on the Plaza del Angel belonging to his uncle, a well-to-do cleric by the name of Diego Lucio Zorrilla. Rojas' residence as a boy on the Plaza del Angel could not have been more propitious for his later career as a dramatist. There he probably received his early education from Pedro Díaz Morante, a Toledan schoolmaster who opened a private school at the same address in 1612. Pedro Calderón de la Barca, Rojas' future collaborator, and his younger brother, José, Rojas' life-long friend, also attended the same school. Nearby was the so-called Quarter of the Muses where the most famous men of Spanish letters lived during Rojas' boyhood—among them, Cervantes, Lope de Vega, and Francisco de Quevedo. And but a block or two from Rojas' home were the two principal theaters, the Príncipe and the Cruz, as well as the Gossip Corner (*Mentidero de los Representantes*), meeting place of poets and painters, actors and playwrights. In his *Keep Your Eyes Open* (*Abre el ojo*) Rojas takes his readers on a guided tour of his adopted city and his own neighborhood.

It is not known where or when Rojas completed his university studies, if indeed he completed them, but presumably he attended the University of Salamanca,[1] the setting of two of his plays, *What the Marquis of Villena Wanted to See* (*Lo que quería ver el Marqués de Villena*) and *Obligated and Offended, and the Freeloader of Salamanca* (*Obligados y ofendidos, y gorrón de Salamanca*). Both plays present an intimate view of student life. Indications are that Rojas shared a room at the university with Antonio Coello, his future collaborator, and with Antonio de Solís, dramatist, chronicler of the Indies, and secretary of Philip IV in later years. Apparently both Coello and Rojas continued to wear their student garb after they became involved in literary circles at the court in the 1630's, since there are numerous contemporary references to the filthy gowns which they had abandoned only recently. Rojas in particular is depicted as having been especially slovenly in his dress.

Rojas' first printed work was a sonnet which was published in October of 1631 in a volume entitled the *Amphitheater of Philip the Great* (*Anfiteatro de Felipe el Grande*), edited by José Pellicer de Tovar. The occasion was an auspicious one for his debut: Philip IV shot and killed a bull which, after having routed several other animals in an exhibition staged in the Plaza del Parque, ran amuck and terrorized the audience. Rojas' laudatory sonnet may not have attracted much attention since eighty-nine Spanish poets are represented in the volume dedicated to immortalizing their monarch's feat, but one thing is significant: both Rojas' first printed work and the last words he wrote (in 1648) are dedicated to Philip IV. The Toledan dramatist, luckily, always enjoyed his sovereign's favor. From the time that he first became active in Spanish letters, he had a prominent role in the literary entertainment presented at the court. Only Calderón surpassed him in his popularity as a court dramatist.

By 1632, when he was twenty-five, Rojas had already acquired a reputation as a playwright, according to Juan Pérez de Montalván, disciple and biographer of Lope de Vega. In his *For Everyone* (*Para todos*), Montalván praises his talents and refers to the applause elicited by "the ingenious plays he has written." [2] Now just what plays, ingenious or otherwise, Rojas had composed by 1632 it is hard to say. The earliest play of his individual composition was long regarded as *Saint Isabel, Queen of Portugal* (*Santa Isabel, reina de Portugal*), recorded by *The Inquirer* (*El Averiguador*) (I, 107) as having been performed in the Royal Palace on September 18, 1631, but there is some question about the date. Cotarelo thought the year should be 1635 instead of 1631, a view which is supported by the fact that the company of Juan Martínez de los Ríos, which performed Rojas' play, is not known to have acted in the Royal Palace before 1633. [3]

At any rate, early in his career Rojas was accepted as a collaborator by some of the most prominent dramatists of the day, including Luis Vélez de Guevara, Calderón, and Montalván. With his school companion, Antonio Coello, and Vélez de Guevara, he wrote *La Baltasara* (dated c. 1630), initiating a partnership that was to endure throughout much of his career. With Calderón and Montalván he wrote *The Prodigy of Fortune, the Laundress of Naples* (*El monstruo de la fortuna y lavandera de Nápoles*), dated c. 1632. Rojas learned much of his craftsmanship from Vélez and Calderón, and although he continued to collaborate with the author of *Life Is a Dream* (*La vida es sueño*), he was soon vying with him for favor in the public theaters and at the court.

Rojas' first independent play of certain date is *Persiles y Segismunda*, a dramatization of Cervantes' posthumous novel, *Persiles y Sigismunda*. It was performed by the troupe of Luis López de Sustaete on February 23, 1633, before the king and queen at the palace, El Pardo. Although Rojas did not succeed in reducing the vast canvas of Cervantes' Byzantine novel to workable proportions, he came up with a tragic melodrama that anticipates one of the most persistent and distinctive traits of his dramaturgy: the violent conclusion to which the good and evil alike fall victim. After subjecting the lovers to many harrowing experiences and having them languish interminably in prison, Rojas, on the very eve of their liberation, has them plunge accidentally to their deaths from a castle wall. Most Spanish dramatists, as Cervantes himself did, would have rewarded the virtuous couple with a triumphant wedding and the prospect of many happy years to come.

By 1635, the year of Lope de Vega's death, Rojas had become firmly entrenched as a favorite court dramatist, since in that year seven of his plays, including two written in collaboration, were performed in the Royal Palace.[4] In the following year, 1636, five more of his plays, including two written in collaboration, were performed before the king and queen.[5] Rojas, it seems, enjoyed the special patronage of the queen, Isabel de Borbón.

The Spanish playwrights who lived under Philip IV were kept too busy churning out entertainment for their royal patrons and the groundlings of the public theaters to be able to indulge in artistic moods. Hence, there are in Rojas' career no well-defined "dark" periods and no "light" ones. Gay comedy and somber tragedy followed each other in haphazard order, and the pot was kept boiling. So it was that on January 29, 1637, before a royal audience at El Pardo, the company of Pedro de la Rosa presented one of Rojas' most delightful comedies, *Dishonor Leaves No Room for Jealousy* (*Donde hay agravios no hay celos*), one of the earliest European plays to employ the device of having master and lackey exchange identities.[6] A little more than two weeks later, on February 14, 1637, came the performance in El Pardo of Rojas' most truculent tragedy, *The Most Unlikely Executioner for the Most Just Revenge* (*El más impropio verdugo por la más justa venganza*). A savage play, it represents the culmination of the father-son conflicts in Rojas' theater, since in the final scenes an outraged father executes his murderous son on the public scaffold. The slashed corpse is exposed to public view. Rojas' play must have been a shocking prelude to the royal festivities which began in Madrid on the following day, February 15.

María de Borbón, princess of Carignan, arrived in Spain for a long visit in November of 1636. The Count-Duke Olivares, chief minister of the king, took advantage of the royal visit to organize a series of festivities which lasted from February 15 to February 24, 1637.[7] At a cost of more than 500,000 ducats the entertainment included tourneys, banquets, masque balls, plays and parades, and other high jinks. One of the plays composed for the occasion was *The Rape of the Sabines* (*El robo de las Sabinas*), written in collaboration by Rojas, Antonio Coello, and Juan Coello. Also, as part of the entertainment, a burlesque literary academy was held, for which Rojas acted as *fiscal* or "prosecutor." Alfonso de Batres wrote the first part of the *vejamen*, a lampoon satirizing the personal qualities of all participants in the academy, and Rojas wrote the second part.[8] After poking fun at his own baldness, Rojas excoriated his fellow poets with zeal.

So well did Rojas carry out his task that on a similar occasion during the following year he was again named to write part of the *vejamen*. The French noblewoman María de Rohan-Montbazon, duchess of Chevreuse, was a guest at the court during the pre-Lenten days of 1638, and once again the Count-Duke Olivares drew heavily upon the flagging Spanish treasury to provide lavish entertainment. As in the preceding year, there was a poetry contest followed by a *vejamen* in charge of Antonio Coello and Alfonso de Batres. At the last minute, however, on the Queen's request and on the orders of the King himself, Rojas was substituted for Batres, choice of the Count-Duke.

Coello's *vejamen* is of interest for its anecdotes concerning Rojas' personal habits during his school days. So filthy was Rojas, says Coello, that whenever he left his residence to go out into the street, a servant cried out "Rojas va," instead of the customary "agua va" ("watch out for the water!") called out as a warning when garbage pails and chamber pots were emptied from upper-story windows into the street.

For his part, Rojas showed his appreciation for being selected to write the *vejamen* by addressing to Philip IV some of the most unabashed flattery ever directed to a Spanish king: "On this great day (fourth planet of Spain) when your sacred ears deign to listen to our human voices, let my voice burst forth and my desire, as far as possible, obtain your attention. Illumine (oh Sun of Europe) my writing with your rays, so that my careless slips may look better. Impel me, sovereign Mars, to contests of wit. Most attentive Jupiter, may the effects of your wisdom flow in me so that my pen may match your lance . . ." [9]

No less flattering but perhaps less banal was the praise addressed to the visiting duchess, to the ladies of the court, and to the Queen ("Isabel de Borbón, who, having been born a lily of France, changed to the color of a beautiful Spanish rose . . !")

But the business of a *vejamen* was to deal out vituperation, not flattery, and Rojas soon got down to the job at hand. The targets for his barbs were many, but none came off so poorly as Alfonso de Batres, who had shared the *vejamen* with him the year before. Apparently, however, not everyone took his jests in fun. On April 24, 1638, one of the contemporary news bulletins (*Avisos*) recorded that Rojas had been murdered; and on May 22, the same source attributed his murder to unnamed persons disgruntled by his scurrilous *vejamen*.[10]

Fortunately, it was all a mistake. Although he was severely wounded, Rojas did not die in 1638. Rather, he spent his convalescence writing one of his most memorable comedies, *Merry Sport with Fools* (*Entre bobos anda el juego*). In this *comedia de figurón* in which several characters are caricatures, Rojas bestowed the name of Wig (*Cabellera*) on the lackey and proceeded to poke fun at bald men. He had not lost his sense of humor.

Like many successful Spanish dramatists, Rojas felt obliged, perhaps because of financial reasons, to try his hand at writing *autos sacramentales* (Sacramental Plays), those peculiarly Spanish allegorical dramas performed publicly in street and square on Corpus Christi Day in celebration of the dogma of the Holy Eucharist. Of the fifteen *autos* attributed to him by Cotarelo, all were presumably composed between 1639 and 1648. During the same period, Calderón (whose superiority in the *auto* Rojas never challenged) is estimated to have written ten or less.[11]

Also composed in 1639 was *Our Lady of Atocha* (*Nuestra Señora de Atocha*), one of the few religious plays, other than the *autos sacramentales*, written by the secular-minded Rojas.

The autograph manuscript of the play, one of his very few autographs still preserved, is dated February 11. I have been unable to discover evidence that it was written for a special occasion, but I suspect that it was. All Spanish sovereigns of the house of Hapsburg were especially devoted to Our Lady of Atocha, but Philip IV, ever torn between dissolution and religiosity, exceeded all his forebears in his devotion to the Patroness of Madrid. It is recorded that by 1659, six years prior to his death, he had made 3,400 visits to the image and that he ordered the Virgin brought to the Royal Palace when he was on his death bed.[12] Rojas was not unmindful of his king's predilection.

On November 21, 1640, Rojas married Doña Catalina Yáñez Trillo de Mendoza, whose father was a councilman in Guadalajara and formerly the city's solicitor in the Cortes. The only issue of this marriage was Antonio Juan de Rojas, born on June 25, 1642, who later became a judge of the Real Audiencia de México where he died sometime before 1694. However, Rojas had an illegitimate daughter, Francisca María de Rojas Zorrilla, born in 1636 of his liaison with the actress María de Escobedo, who was married—much to the consternation of the dramatist's biographers—to a comedian also named Francisco de Rojas. After the death of María de Escobedo in 1642, Rojas placed his daughter in the care of his illegitimate half-brother Gregorio de Rojas, an actor who had assumed the stage name Juan Bezón. The daughter also chose a stage career, becoming a leading actress under the name of Francisca Bezón, and later the manager of a theatrical company. She died in 1704.[13]

In 1640 Rojas supervised the publication of Part I of his plays, printed by the firm of María de Quiñones, at the expense of the bookseller Pedro Coello, to whom the rights had been sold. On February 4 of the same year, Rojas' play based on the story of Romeo and Juliet, *The Rival Houses of Verona* (*Los bandos de Verona*), was chosen to inaugurate the Coliseo, a lavish theater in the park of the Buen Retiro engineered by the Italian architect, Cosme Lotti. Stage machinery there had long been in the Spanish theaters, but the Coliseo, with its movable scenery, elaborate apparatus and accessory gadgets, was to put a high premium on the ingenuity of playwrights in achieving

FRANCISCO DE ROJAS ZORRILLA

the spectacular. On July 2 a play of unknown title written in collaboration by Rojas, Calderón, and Antonio de Solís was also performed in the Coliseo.[14]

Although none of Rojas' plays, other than the *autos sacramentales*, has been definitely dated after 1640, it may be presumed that his production continued apace until 1644. In March of that year, enemies of the theater managed to convince Spanish officialdom that the ills besetting the country were attributable in part to the moral laxity of the stage. Accordingly, a decree was issued providing that "henceforth no *comedia* which is the author's own invention may be performed, but only *historias* or lives of saints." [15] This prohibition appears not to have been strictly enforced until the death of the queen, Isabel de Borbón, on October 6, 1644, at which time all public spectacles were suspended. During the period of mourning the enemies of the theater renewed their attacks, and their cause was abetted when Prince Baltasar Carlos died in Zaragoza on October 9, 1646. The theaters remained closed until 1649, although special permission was occasionally granted for the presentation of *autos sacramentales*. Unlike most Spanish playwrights, Rojas had no other profession to fall back on. He took advantage of his enforced leisure to publish Part II of his plays, printed in 1645 at his own expense, and to engage in litigation in which he had a special interest.

In 1643 Philip IV, grateful to Rojas for his services as a court dramatist, nominated him for membership in the Order of Santiago. Accordingly, the Council of Orders designated representatives to make the customary investigations pertaining to purity of blood. Their reports could not have been more discomfiting to one who aspired to the habit of Santiago. Rojas, it was alleged, not only was tainted by Moorish blood but had Jewish ancestors on both sides of his family, some of whom were sentenced to execution by the Inquisition. One of the investigators concluded his report of October 11, 1644 by charging that although Rojas had bribed witnesses, it was clear that his ancestors were converted Jews and that "in Toledo everybody knows that the Zorrillas and Chiribogas were (converted Jews), although they may give them habits of all the (military) orders." [16]

Although the Count-Duke Olivares had been dismissed in 1643, he still had powerful friends at court, and it did not help Rojas' chances that his kinsman Francisco de Chiriboga, inspired by visions, was one of the first to bring charges of malfeasance in office against Olivares.[17]

As proceedings dragged on, Rojas, embarrassed but determined, wrote a crisp letter to the king requesting action. At the insistence of the king, Francisco de Quevedo was appointed to expedite matters.[18] Himself a member of the Order of Santiago and a friend of Rojas, Quevedo managed to gain the support of the Consejo, although that body did not issue its official approval until October 13, 1645. Papal dispensation having been secured to free the candidate from the impediment that his father had once exercised gainful employment as a notary, Rojas was able to don his habit.

In 1647 Rojas was called upon to compose an *auto sacramental* when permission was granted to present the Corpus Christi celebrations in Madrid. That such permission was granted at the last moment is made clear by a passage in Jerónimo Cáncer's *loa sacramental* which accompanied Rojas' *The Great Courtyard of the Palace* (*El gran patio de palacio*): "Don Francisco de Rojas, who is the author of this, wrote it in three days, which is a good excuse if by chance it is not good."[19]

Rojas improvised a wooden, spiritless piece, but despite its clumsiness, *El gran patio de palacio* is not without interest. Here is an allegory (whether Rojas intended it to be or not) of Philip's court. The great courtyard of the Royal Palace—once thronged with actors and actresses, poets and buffoons, the scene of *soirées* and masques and literary contests—had become but weeping walls for the morbid king. The palace is besieged by malcontents and fakers, including those who want to be members of the military orders "and go about sowing genealogies."[20] Strange words from a man who had been accused of bribing witnesses to give false testimony about his ancestry! Philip's court and its hangers-on had fallen on foul days indeed.

The last words Rojas is known to have written—his epitaph as dramatist—are the closing lines of *El gran patio de palacio,* addressed to Philip IV.

And Don Francisco de Rojas   18
begs of your Royal Majesty
to pardon him, knowing
that you always pardon.[21]

Perhaps the victim of foul play like that which almost claimed
his life a decade earlier, Rojas died (with the benefit of the
Holy Sacraments but too suddenly to make a will) on January
23, 1648. He was in his forty-first year.

CHAPTER 2

The Plays: Problems

I The Problem of Authenticity

IN ATTEMPTING to classify Rojas' plays, one is immediately confronted, as in the case of many Golden Age dramatists, with the problem of the authenticity of the plays attributed to him. Rojas never compiled a catalogue of titles such as Lope de Vega included in his *Pilgrim in His Own Country* (*El peregrino en su patria*) (1604), or such as Calderón sent to the Duke of Veragua in 1680, a year before his death. Although Lope's list is incomplete and Calderón's leaves unanswered several questions concerning his authorship, they at least provide a point of departure. With Rojas we are not so fortunate.

Like many prominent dramatists of his time, Rojas was plagued by having plays by unknown authors published under his name, a practice which he asserts led him to publish his Part II (*Segunda parte*, Madrid, 1645): "To the reader: in Seville they print the plays of the least known authors under the name of those who have written most. If the play is good, they usurp the praise due its author; if it is bad, they detract from the reputation of the one who did not write it. Some two weeks ago I passed by the steps of Trinity Church, and among other plays which they were selling there was the title of one: *The Follies of Love* (*Los desatinos de amor*) by Don Francisco de Rojas. Aren't my own follies enough, I said, without their baptizing those of other people with my name? I decided for this reason to go on with this printing . . ."

There is another factor which has contributed to the confusion of Rojas' bibliographers: his name. Francisco de Rojas was a common name in seventeenth-century Spain, and frequently the second surname of authors was omitted in their printed works. At least three other men by the name of Francisco de Rojas are known to have written plays during our author's lifetime; another, ironically, was a vitriolic enemy of the theater.[1] It is entirely possible that some of the plays associated with the Toledan dramatist were composed by one or more of his lesser known contemporaries.

Mesonero Romanos, who first addressed himself to the task of compiling a catalogue of Rojas' titles, summarized his findings in these words: "It turns out, then, that there appears under Rojas' name a repertory of some eighty plays (although some are evidently false and others are presumably so), including the plays written in collaboration."[2] Mesonero's doubt about the authenticity of some of these eighty plays was well-founded indeed.

In his turn, Cotarelo lists seventy full-length plays, including twelve written in collaboration, as being of Rojas' authorship, although he makes clear that twelve titles were known only through an advertisement in a catalogue of an eighteenth-century bookseller: Francisco Medel, *Indice general alfabético de todos los títulos de comedias que se han escrito por varios autores antiguos y modernos . . .* (Madrid, 1735). In addition, Cotarelo includes the titles of fifteen *autos* and two interludes (*entremeses*) as Rojas', but rejects twenty-one plays as being apochryphal or doubtful. Although Cotarelo's conclusions are based almost exclusively on bibliographical and external data, rather than on a study of versification and internal evidence, his investigations have been very fruitful.

Less reliable is one of Rojas' more recent editors, F. Ruiz Morcuende, who lists the titles of eighty-eight plays, *autos*, and *entremeses* as being "unquestionably Rojas'."[3] However, ten of these titles are known only through their inclusion in Medel's catalogue, and eight others have been questioned by other students of Rojas.

In point of fact, we can be sure of the authenticity of few plays attributed to Rojas other than the twenty-four contained in the two *Partes* of 1640 and 1645, although it is reasonable to assume that he wrote considerably more.[4] Only two of his autograph, or partially autograph, manuscripts are preserved, but both plays in question, *Remedies Involve Risks* (*Peligrar en los remedios*) and *Our Lady of Atocha* (*Nuestra Señora de Atocha*), are printed in the *Partes*. Contemporary references (contained in printed news bulletins, letters, and booking contracts) to the performance of plays written solely by Rojas or in collaboration account for twenty-two titles, but all but one title of his individual authorship, *To Each His Due* (*Cada cual lo que le toca*), are contained in the *Partes*.

The twenty-four plays printed in the two *Partes*, prepared for publication by Rojas himself, tell us enough about his practices and patterns of versification to make us wary of the authenticity of any play that deviates radically from the norm. Despite his penchant for tragic endings, Rojas was always lavish in his treatment of comic scenes. His concern with the comic begins with the name of the clown (*gracioso*) to which he pays close attention (as do some other Golden Age dramatists). Of the twenty-four plays in the *Partes*, twenty-one have *graciosos* with common nouns for names—Moscón (Big Fly), Coscorrón (Bump), Bofetón (Bop), etc.—which become the object of elaborate punning. In two of the other three plays Rojas was up to other tricks. In *Dishonor Leaves No Room for Jealousy* (*Donde hay agravios no hay celos*) Sancho is named after Don Quijote's squire because of his misadventures with his own master. In *The Most Unlikely Executioner for the Most Just Revenge* (*El más impropio verdugo por la más justa venganza*) Cosme and Damián are named for the inseparable brother saints whose intimate association they parody. Neither of Rojas' clowns can go to the bathroom without the other's company. In all but two plays the *gracioso* is present in the final scene. In *Obligated and Offended* (*Obligados y ofendidos*) Crispinillo leaves in the next to the last scene, and in *Remedies Involve Risks* (*Peligrar en los remedios*) Bofetón and Celia make a point of taking leave of the audience before they quit the stage.

Rojas usually followed the convention of having the *gracioso* speak the final lines, but no matter who speaks them, the twenty-four plays, with one exception, conform to one or the other of two stereotypes. The one exception is *Saint Isabel, Queen of Portugal* (*Santa Isabel, reina de Portugal*) in which the *gracioso* promises a second part. In six plays the author's spokesman, usually the *gracioso*, asks for the spectators' *perdón*; in seventeen he solicits a "hurrah" (*vítor*) for the author. Rennert remarks, not without reason, that Rojas was the most shameless of all Golden Age dramatists in persistently begging for applause.[5] As a matter of related interest, in the latter part of his career Rojas often inserted his own name in the final verses. None of the twelve plays in the first *Parte* contains his name in the closing lines, but eight in the second *Parte* do. Rojas became a believer in self-advertising.

Four verse forms—*romance, redondillas, silvas,* and *décimas*—are characteristic of the great majority of Rojas' plays.[6] Any play that lacks one of the forms (except *décimas*, which are not contained in six plays in the *Partes*) must be held suspect. Like several other dramatists of Calderón's generation, Rojas greatly favored ballad meter, the *romance*. The plays in the two *Partes* average 64 percent *romance*, the highest percentage (78) being found in *Medea's Sorcery* (*Los encantos de Medea*) and the lowest (38) in *Progne y Filomena*. The second most common meter is *redondillas* which average between 25 and 30 percent in the twenty-four plays, the highest being found in *Obligados y ofendidos* (49) and the lowest, 9, in *To Marry for Revenge* (*Casarse por vengarse*). *Silvas* are found in all but two of the plays, *Honor Weighs More Than Friendship* (*No hay amigo para amigo*) and *The Trials of Tobias* (*Los trabajos de Tobías*) but average less than 10 percent. *Décimas* are employed in eighteen of the plays but average less than 5 percent in the plays in which they occur.

Other verse forms are conspicuous by their absence or rarity in the *Partes*. None of the twenty-four plays contains *liras,* tercets or royal octaves; only one contains *seguidillas, The Ways of Women* (*Lo que son mujeres*); only two have sonnets (*Persiles y Segismunda* and *Lo que son mujeres*); and only three employ *quintillas, Cleopatra's Serpents* (*Los áspides de Cleopatra*) *The Cain of Catalonia* (*El Caín de Cataluña*), and *The Trials of Tobias* (*Los trabajos de Tobías*).

Of course, some of the plays not published in the *Partes* but whose authorship seems beyond question do not adhere strictly to the characteristic verse distribution. Such a play is *Numantia Destroyed* (*Numancia destruída*) which contains more or less the "proper" percentage of *romance, redondillas, silvas,* and *décimas* (48.7, 15.7, 6.7, and 4.9 percent, respectively), but which also employs several meters which I have called gratuitous (*quintillas*, 12.4 percent; royal octaves, 5.7; *liras*, 3.2; *sextillas*, 1.13; sonnet, .53; and *canción*, .45 percent). Quite a different case is presented, however, by *Below the King All Men Are Peers* (*Del rey abajo, ninguno*), long regarded as Rojas' masterpiece, whose authorship I have questioned elsewhere.[7] Not only does this play contain several uncharacteristic meters but it also deviates sharply in the proportion and distribution of the usual forms. However, I also regard it as questionable because of uncharacteristic dramaturgical traits which need not be detailed here.

In addition to the twenty-four plays printed in the two *Partes*, of which *The Three Glories of Spain* (*Los tres blasones de España*) was written in collaboration with Antonio Coello, the texts of other plays are preserved in manuscript, in single printed editions (*sueltas*), or in general collections of plays of various seventeenth-century authors. Below is a list of titles showing: A. Authentic Plays of Individual Authorship; B. Plays Written in Collaboration; and C. Authentic *autos sacramentales*. The thirty-five titles listed in section A are followed by the number I or II indicating that the play was printed in Rojas' *Parte primera* (1640) or *Parte segunda* (1645), or by the letters M, S, or C, in parentheses indicating that the text is preserved in manuscript, in a *suelta*, or in a general collection of plays. Of course, some plays are preserved in various seventeenth-century versions, both in manuscript and print, but in such cases I have indicated only one version. More complete information, including bibliographical data on all known editions of his plays, can be found in Cotarelo and in my monograph, *Francisco de Rojas Zorrilla: bibliografía crítica* (Madrid, 1965).

A. Authentic Plays of Individual Authorship

1. *Abrir el ojo* (*Keep Your Eyes Open*), II
2. *Aspides* (*Los*) *de Cleopatra* (*Cleopatra's Serpents*), II
3. *Bandos* (*Los*) *de Verona* (*The Rival Houses of Verona*), II
4. *Cada cual lo que le toca* (*To Each His Due*), M
5. *Caín* (*El*) *de Cataluña* (*The Cain of Catalonia*), C
6. *Casarse por vengarse* (*To Marry for Revenge*), I

7. *Celos (Los) de Rodamonte (Rodamonte's Jealousy)*, I
8. *Desafío (El) de Carlos V (The Duel of Charles V)*, S
9. *Donde hay agravios no hay celos (Dishonor Leaves No Room for Jealousy)*, I
10. *Encantos (Los) de Medea (Medea's Sorcery)*, II
11. *Entre bobos anda el juego (Merry Sport with Fools)*, II
12. *Lo que quería ver el Marqués de Villena (What the Marquis of Villena Wanted to See)*, II
13. *Lo que son mujeres (The Ways of Women)*, II
14. *Lucrecia y Tarquino (Lucretia and Tarquin)*, S
15. *Más (El) impropio verdugo por la más justa venganza (The Most Unlikely Executioner for the Most Just Revenge)*, II
16. *Mejor (El) amigo el muerto y capuchino escocés (The Dead Man as the Best Friend, or the Scotch Capuchin)*, M
17. *Morir pensando matar (To Die Intending to Kill)*, C
18. *No hay amigo para amigo (Honor Weighs More Than Friendship)*, I
19. *No hay duelo entre dos amigos (Friends Don't Duel)*, S
20. *No hay ser padre siendo rey (A King Cannot Act as a Father)*, I
21. *Nuestra Señora de Atocha (Our Lady of Atocha)*, II
22. *Numancia cercada (Numantia Besieged)*, M
23. *Numancia destruída (Numantia Destroyed)*, S
24. *Obligados y ofendidos y gorrón de Salamanca (Obligated and Offended, and the Freeloader of Salamanca)*, I
25. *Peligrar en los remedios (Remedies Involve Risks)*, I
26. *Persiles y Segismunda (Persiles and Segismunda)*, I
27. *Primer Marqués (El) de Astorga (The First Marquis of Astorga)*, M
28. *Primero es la honra que el gusto (Honor Comes Before Pleasure)*, S
29. *Profeta (El) falso Mahoma (The False Prophet Mohammed)*, I
30. *Progne y Filomena (Procne and Philomela)*, I
31. *Santa Isabel, reina de Portugal (Saint Isabel, Queen of Portugal)*, I
32. *Sin honra no hay amistad (Without Honor There Can Be No Friendship)*, II
33. *Trabajos (Los) de Tobías (The Trials of Tobias)*, II

34. *Traición* (*La*) *busca el castigo* (*Treason Seeks Its Own Punishment*), I
35. *Vida* (*La*) *en el ataúd* (*Life Is Found in the Coffin*), C

B. Plays Written in Collaboration

(The names of the collaborators are given in the order of the authorship of each act.)

1. *Baltasara* (*La*) (Luis Vélez de Guevara, Antonio Coello, and Rojas)
2. *Bandolero* (*El*) *Solposto* (*The Bandit Solposto*) (Jerónimo Cáncer, Pedro Rosete Niño, and Rojas)
3. *Catalán* (*El*) *Serrallonga* (*Serrallonga the Catalonian*) (Antonio Coello, Rojas, and Vélez de Guevara)
4. *Jardín* (*El*) *de Falerina* (*The Garden of Falerina*) (Rojas, Antonio Coello, and Calderón)
5. *Más* (*La*) *hidalga hermosura* (*The Most Noble Beauty*) (Juan de Zabaleta, Rojas, and Calderón)
6. *Mejor* (*El*) *amigo el muerto* (*y fortunas de don Juan de Castro*) (*The Dead Man as the Best Friend*) (*and the Fortunes of Don Juan de Castro*) (Luis de Belmonte, Rojas, and Calderón. This play is not to be confused with the play of Rojas' individual authorship, *El mejor amigo el muerto y capuchino escocés*.)
7. *Monstruo* (*El*) *de la fortuna* (*La lavandera de Nápoles*) (*The Prodigy of Fortune, the Laundress of Naples*) (probably Calderón, Juan Pérez de Montalbán, and Rojas, although there is some question concerning Rojas' collaborators)
8. *Pleito* (*El*) *del demonio con la Virgen* (*The Contest of the Devil with the Virgin*) (a manuscript and early printed editions attribute this play to *tres ingenios* but Rojas may have written the whole.)
9. *Pleito* (*El*) *que tuvo el diablo con el cura de Madrilejos* (*The Contest of the Devil with the Priest of Madrilejos*) (Vélez de Guevara, Rojas, and perhaps Mira de Amescua)
10. *Robo* (*El*) *de las Sabinas* (*The Rape of the Sabines*) (Rojas,

Juan Coello, and Antonio Coello, although Rojas may also have had a hand in the second act)

11. *También la afrenta es veneno* (*An Insult Can Also Be Poisonous*) (Vélez de Guevara, Antonio Coello, and Rojas)
12. *También tiene el sol menguante* (*The Sun Also Wanes*) (Vélez de Guevara and Rojas)
13. *Tres* (*Los*) *blasones de España* (*The Three Glories of Spain*) (Antonio Coello, Act I, and Rojas)
14. *Trompeta* (*La*) *del juicio* (*The Horn of Judgment Day*) (Gabriel del Corral and Rojas?)
15. *Villano* (*El*) *gran señor y gran Tamorlán de Persia* (*The Lordly Peasant, Tambourlaine the Great of Persia*) (Rojas, Jerónimo de Villanueva, and Gabriel de Roa)

C. Authentic *autos sacramentales*

1. *Acreedores* (*Los*) *del hombre* (*Man's Creditors*)
2. *Ferias* (*Las*) *de Madrid* (*The Fairs of Madrid*) (nonextant but known to be Rojas' through contemporary references)
3. *Galán valiente y discreto* (*Gallant, Brave, and Discreet*)
4. *Gran* (*El*) *patio de palacio* (*The Great Courtyard of the Palace*)
5. *Hércules* (*El*) (*Hercules*)
6. *Rico* (*El*) *avariento* (*The Rich Man*)
7. *Sansón* (*Samson*) (non-extant but known to be Rojas' through contemporary references)
8. *Sotillo* (*El*) *de Madrid* (*The Grove of Madrid*) (non-extant but known to be Rojas' through contemporary references)
9. *Viña* (*La*) *de Nabot* (*Nabot's Vineyard*)

Rojas is also credited with the authorship of one interlude, *El doctor,* but his claim to another, *The Trifling Mayor* (*El alcalde Ardite*), has been disputed.[8]

II *The Problem of Classification*

Although of a different order, the problems arising from an attempt to classify Rojas' plays—indeed, the plays of any major

Golden Age dramatist—are no less vexatious than the problems of authenticity. More than a century ago George Ticknor despaired of the task of making a meaningful classification of Calderón's plays, because ". . . in the great majority of cases, the boundaries of no class are respected; and in many of them even more than two forms of the drama melt imperceptibly into each other. Especially in those pieces whose subjects are taken from known history, sacred or profane, or from the recognized fictions of mythology or romance, there is frequently a confusion that seems as though it were intended to set all classifications at defiance." [9]

In effect, what Ticknor did (long before the word "baroque" became fashionable) was to give a good definition of baroque drama—a type of drama in which two or more forms "melt imperceptibly into each other." Whether dealing with the plays of Lope or Calderón or Rojas, one can no longer speak, as Polonius does in *Hamlet*, of "tragedy, comedy, history, pastoral, pastoral-comical, historical-pastoral, scene individable, or poem unlimited" (Act III, sc. 2). The fact is that baroque plays are "poems unlimited," and only nitwits, some critics contend, would do more than analyze the form of each individual "poem."

It is not enough, however, to say that all of Rojas' plays are baroque, that they defy classification into traditional types, and let it go at that. Of all the plays ascribed to Rojas, only *Del rey abajo, ninguno* has received much critical attention and has been subjected to efforts to define its form. The other plays beg attention, but we cannot analyze them all in depth. Rather, we must generalize on them, giving greater care to the better ones and slighting the lesser ones. An old-fashioned classification will help in making the generalizations.

One of the most complete classifications of Rojas' theater is found in Hurtado and Palencia, *Historia de la literatura española,* 5th ed. (Madrid, 1943), p. 686, where twenty-five plays are classified under six major divisions: Religious, Historical, Manners and Customs, Novelistic, Chivalresque, and Mythological (*Religiosas, Históricas, De costumbres, Novelescas, Caballerescas,* and *Mitológicas*) and eleven sub-divisions. It is, on the whole, a sensible and useful classification.

Less complete but satisfactory as far as it goes is the classification of Angel Valbuena, *Literatura dramática española* (Barcelona, 1930), p. 255, who divides twelve plays into two main categories, Tragedies and Plays of Contemporary Customs (Cape-and-Sword Plays) (*Género trágico* and *Género de costumbres contemporáneas* [*de capa y espada*]), and six sub-divisions. In reducing Rojas' plays to two major genres, Valbuena, it appears, anticipates Pfandl's words about the Toledan: "As a dramatic author he merits special consideration in that he possessed for his time an extraordinary sense of the distinction between the tragic and the comic. In fact, he is the only one in whose production the tragedies can be distinguished from the comedies."[10] If Pfandl's affirmation were entirely so, the task of classification would be simple, but unfortunately it is at best a half-truth, for Rojas too has many plays in which two or more forms "melt imperceptibly into each other."

Quite apart from the argument that baroque plays cannot be grouped neatly into tragedies and comedies is the fact that all previous classifications of Rojas' plays violate the first principle of classification, that is, classifying according to a common criterion, whether that criterion be theme, predominant motif, the nature of the conflict, or whatnot. Perhaps this violation of principle is not inevitable, but I too have resorted to a classification by more or less traditional types, including the following major divisions: Tragedies, Honor Dramas, Religious Plays, Novelistic Plays, Cape-and-Sword Plays, and Plays of Manners and Customs.

TRAGEDIES

Los áspides de Cleopatra
Los encantos de Medea
Lucrecia y Tarquino
Progne y Filomena
Morir pensando matar
No hay ser padre siendo rey
El Caín de Cataluña
El más impropio verdugo por la más justa venganza
Numancia cercada
Numancia destruída

HONOR DRAMAS

Del rey abajo, ninguno
Casarse por vengarse
Peligrar en los remedios
Cada cual lo que le toca
La traición busca el castigo

RELIGIOUS PLAYS

Los trabajos de Tobías
El mejor amigo el muerto
Santa Isabel, reina de Portugal
La vida en el ataúd
Nuestra Señora de Atocha
El profeta falso Mahoma
Autos sacramentales (titles listed on p. 32)

NOVELISTIC PLAYS

Persiles y Segismunda
Los celos de Rodamonte
El desafío de Carlos V
El primer Marqués de Astorga
Los bandos de Verona

CAPE-AND-SWORD PLAYS

Donde hay agravios no hay celos
No hay amigo para amigo
No hay duelo entre dos amigos
Obligados y ofendidos, y gorrón de Salamanca
Primero es la honra que el gusto
Sin honra no hay amistad

PLAYS OF MANNERS AND CUSTOMS

Abre el ojo
Lo que son mujeres
Lo que quería ver el Marqués de Villena
Entre bobos anda el juego (*comedia de figurón*)

CHAPTER 3

The Tragedies

WHEN Lope de Vega shaped the new *comedia* toward the end of the sixteenth century, he used the precedents of his precursors as an excuse for his own departures from the "rules of art," but it was primarily he, with his thousand and more plays, who was responsible for the irrevocable break with classical dramaturgy. As in the case of the Elizabethan playwrights, he violated every classical precept. He mixed tragic and comic elements profusely (if not indiscriminately), he made the high- and low-born rub elbows, he admitted a wide variety of feeling and experience into the same play.

Lope was not only the great Spanish popularizer of "open form" romantic drama; he was also one of its most articulate apologists and theorists. "Let the tragic and the comic be mixed, and Terence with Seneca," he proclaimed in his *New Art of Writing Plays in This Epoch* (*Arte nuevo de hacer comedias en este tiempo*) (1609), a doctrine which he justifies on the grounds that nature (which most writers at that time still claimed to imitate) owes its beauty to its variety.[1] And so was born a new theory, based on a new esthetic, to "explain" the new *comedia*. It became academic to speak of tragedy and comedy, just, as a matter of fact, it became academic to write tragedies and comedies, as these terms were previously understood. *Comedia* became the generic word for "play," for any and every type of play, although Lope and his disciples found it difficult at times to adjust to the indiscrete term. It was one thing to write a *comedia* which mixed the tragic and the comic, another to know what to call it. Tragicomedy, perhaps?

The Valencian dramatist who wrote under the name of Ricardo de Turia (pseudonym of Pedro Juan de Rejaule y

Toledo?) says in defense of the Lopean *comedia* in his *Apologético de las comedias españolas* (1616):

> . . . no *comedia* of all those performed in Spain is really a comedy but rather tragicomedy, which is a mixture made up of the comic and the tragic. From the latter are taken the lofty characters, the grand action, the terror and pity; and from the former come the private affairs, the laughter, and the jokes. No one considers this mixture improper, since it is not contrary to nature or to the art of poetry for both high and low characters to appear together in the same plot . . .[2]

But as if he were uneasy over his use of the word "tragicomedy," Ricardo de Turia then insists that the *comedia* is not a compound but a blend or mixture, and he draws on Aristotle's first *De Generatione* to explain the difference: ". . . in a blend the parts lose their form and make a third, very different matter, and in a compound, each part is preserved as it was before, without change or mutation."[3] This observation, of course, anticipates Ticknor's remark that in many Spanish *comedias* two or more forms "melt imperceptibly into each other."

Not all Spaniards (especially academic-minded critics) were happy with the new *comedia*. A denunciation of the hybrid form came from two quarters in 1617: from Cristóbal Suárez de Figueroa's *El pasajero* and from Francisco Cascales' *Tablas poéticas*. But in urging a return to the sharp division between tragedy and comedy, these critics were wasting their breath in trying to stem the tide of the Lopean *comedia*.[4]

Lope himself, however, did not hesitate to apply the term "tragedy" (or "tragicomedy") to his plays when he felt they fit that designation, although he makes some interesting qualifications.[5] In 1631, about the time that Rojas began writing for the stage, he completed his honor drama *Punishment Without Vengeance* (*El castigo sin venganza*). In the first printed edition (1634) he wrote in the prologue: ". . . this tragedy was performed only one day at the court . . . it is written in the Spanish style (not in the manner of Greek antiquity or Latin severity), avoiding ghosts, messengers, and choruses; because taste can change precepts, as usage can change clothing and as time can change customs."[6]

Most modern critics have seized upon Lope's words to give a label to all honor plays which end with bloody vengeance: they are tragedies "written in Spanish style." This is well and good, but I see no reason why other plays of serious theme, prevalent somber mood, and "unhappy" conclusion should not, despite their admixture of tragic and comic elements, violation of the unities, and avoidance of "ghosts, messengers, and choruses," be called tragedies "written in Spanish style." I do not share the scruples of a distinguished contemporary critic who thinks that the terms "tragedy" and "comedy" are too loose (or too tight) to be applied to Golden Age plays, preferring to call them *comedias serias* and *comedias farsas*, although "The *comedia seria* can approach Greco-Roman 'tragedy' or can be what Diderot called 'drame.'" [7]

Rojas, like Lope de Vega and Shakespeare, did not write tragedies of classical form. He wrote a number of plays of tragic plot, always liberally interspersed with comic elements, whose total effect can be termed "tragic." I call such plays tragedies—tragedies "written in Spanish style," if you will.

Ever since Alberto Lista remarked more than a century ago on Rojas' special gifts for tragedy, criticism has accorded him a preeminence in that genre rivaled by none of his Spanish contemporaries, or at best only by Calderón. Among other nineteenth-century critics, Ticknor, Ochoa, Schack, and especially la Barrera seconded the opinion of Lista, the only dissenting voice being that of Mesonero Romanos.[8] The latter, while praising *Del rey abajo, ninguno*, believed that Rojas' abiding merit lay not in the realm of tragedy but in comedy.[9]

In general, critics of the twentieth century have echoed the majority opinion of their predecessors. Menéndez y Pelayo speaks only incidentally of Rojas, but he too holds that Rojas displayed a special bent for tragedy, matched or surpassed only by Calderón; while Cotarelo, Valbuena Prat, and Sáinz de Robles reiterate the vigor of the Toledan's tragic muse.[10] However, the most categorical statement pertaining to Rojas' superiority in the tragedy is that made by Hurtado y Palencia, who affirm that of all Spanish dramatists he possessed in the highest degree a sense of the tragic, and, moreover, in *Los áspides de Cleopatra*, "he shows himself to be the only one in the seventeenth century who had a tragic sense." [11]

Perhaps it would be well to begin the examination of Rojas' tragedies by considering first those of classical theme, since they include subjects which have attracted writers of tragedy in many ages and countries.

I *The Tragedies of Classical Theme*

Rojas' four tragedies drawn from classical history or mythology (*Los áspides de Cleopatra, Los encantos de Medea, Lucrecia y Tarquino,* and *Progne y Filomena*) have several elements in common other than the vintage of their sources. All four have revenge, in varying degree, as an important dramatic motive, and all cast women—Rojas' usual breed of strong-willed women —in the role of revengers. Not only do they differ in their plots, however, but they range in tone and mood from the shrillness of melodrama to the poignancy of classical tragedy.

Los áspides de Cleopatra

Rojas' tragedy was first printed in the *Segunda parte* of his plays (1645), although its date of composition and the date of its first performance are not known. If, however, Alonso de Castillo Solórzano's *Historia de Marco Antonio y Cleopatra, última reina de Egipto* (Zaragoza, 1639) is one of its sources, as may well be the case, it is one of Rojas' later plays.

Los áspides de Cleopatra would seem to invite comparison with Shakespeare's *Antony and Cleopatra* because they both treat the same subject and both derive, in part at least, from Plutarch.[12] In some respects, however, Rojas' tragedy resembles *Romeo and Juliet* more closely, since his Marco Antonio and Cleopatra are a couple of innocents, a "pair of star-crossed lovers" who cannot resist their adverse fate.

In the first act of *Los áspides de Cleopatra,* Lépido, Octaviano, and Marco Antonio return separately to Rome to report on their campaigns in the far reaches of the globe. Octaviano had promised his sister Irene in marriage to the most successful of his fellow triumvirs. The three recount their fortunes. Lépido was defeated on the sea by Cleopatra, and is scorned by Irene because of his loss. Antonio receives a hero's welcome (and Irene's hand) because of his victories in Asia. Octaviano was humbled on the battlefield by Cleopatra and lost his heart to her in the bargain: "My eyes sailed/ the waves of her hair/ and I drowned in her beauty." [13] Marco Antonio reproves Octaviano for his weakness but promises to subdue Cleopatra and lay her heart at his friend's feet. He cannot tarry long enough to marry Irene.

The scene shifts to Egypt where Cleopatra, far different from Shakespeare's tawny-breasted gypsy, is called the "sole symbol of her own purity." And pure she is indeed. She condemns a woman who has sinned against chastity to be poisoned by asps, and remains undaunted when the victim invokes on her a curse that she also fall in love and die in the same manner. Moments later Marco Antonio arrives, bent on subduing the Egyptian "sun." Their eyes meet. Both are blinded by love.

Act II begins a year later with the arrival of Octaviano and Irene, who come to "rescue" Antonio, from whom they have received no news. Caimán, a Roman soldier, tells them that Antonio, loyal to Octaviano at first, had taken to the sea to escape Cleopatra's eyes, but she overtook him in a galley bedecked with all the gleaming finery of the Orient. Their confrontation became a tryst of love. Now convinced of Antonio's unfaithfulness, brother and sister resolve to avenge themselves on the lovers.

Persuaded by their followers that they must part, Antonio and Cleopatra come to say goodbye, but at the sight of each other, their resolutions give way to love. Cleopatra, who now says that "she hears through her eyes" and "sees through her ears" ("because love is completely delirious") recalls their first night together. When Octaviano and Irene lay siege to the city, they hear the musicians sing:

> The Venus of Alexandria   18
> and the happiest Roman
> are drinking each other's souls
> through their eyes, in love's rites.
> He betrayed the faith and honor

of Octaviano, his friend,
because, since love is blind,
it does not see friendship either.[14]

This is an explicit statement of the most recurrent theme of
the play: blinded by love, men lose sight of their obligations.

In Act III Octaviano and Irene capture the lovers, but Lépido,
still holding a grudge against the brother and sister for thwart-
ing his love, allows them to escape. Separated during the night,
they search for each other in vain. Believing Cleopatra has
thrown herself into the sea to elude her pursuers, Antonio stabs
himself. Moments later Cleopatra comes across the body of her
lover. Now that the "sun which beautified the earth" has been
eclipsed (Antonio and his honor), she takes an asp from a flower
and, remembering the woman's curse, applies it to her arm.

As Rojas conceived and wrote *Los áspides de Cleopatra*, it
is a romantic tragedy of love—the tragic tale of those who "loved
not wisely but too well." Divesting his play of the political
motivations which traditionally provide the context in which
the lovers' demise is set, Rojas has them fall victim—ostensibly
at least—to Octaviano's and Irene's thirst for vengeance, since
Antonio has violated the sacred bonds of friendship and spurned
the haughty Irene's love. Ironically, however, it is the lovers'
own concupiscence which brings about their fall, because Antonio, who earlier rebuked Octaviano for falling in love with the
Egyptian queen, and Cleopatra, the defender of chastity who
was the "sole symbol of her own purity," become enslaved by
their own passions.

Throughout the play, Rojas tries to capture the splendor of
Cleopatra's court and the opulence of the East by repeating
images of sun and light, of water and sound, of flowers and
aroma. These are heady images that lull the spirit and seduce the
senses. The imagery is intended to illuminate one meaning
that Rojas meant the play to have—a meaning summed up in
a stanza of Wordsworth's *Expostulation and Reply:*

The eye—it cannot choose but see; 18
We cannot bid the ear be still;
Our bodies feel, where'er they be,
Against or with our will.

But this is not all, because the main theme of the play is a moral
one. Man may not be able to repress his senses but he must
learn to control his passions. Otherwise he invites destruction.
The "fate" which overtakes Antonio and Cleopatra is their
failure to dominate *amor ciego* ("blind love").

Los encantos de Medea

This play is based on the familiar story of Jason and Medea,
dramatized by Euripides and Seneca, and related by Ovid in
Book VII of the *Metamorphoses*. It is a story, one would think,
that would have provided grist for Rojas' mill since its central
character is a passionate, vengeful female of the type around
which he loved to spin his plots, and it contains all the ingredients
necessary for an awesome revenge tragedy. For this reason, of
course, it has always been a favorite subject of revenge dramatists
everywhere.

Instead of focussing upon the raw human emotions of his
tormented protagonist, however, Rojas chose to stress (as the
title of his play indicates) the gaudy theatrics of Medea's
sorcery. The stage directions call for, among other things, a
flying cloud, an earthquake, a crumbling mountain, and various
aerial flights. There seems to be little doubt that Rojas fully
intended his play to be a *comedia de magia*, one which would
indeed put to test all the stage machinery available in any
Spanish theater of the times. To top it off, the play contains a
comic subplot involving the servants Mosquete and Mosqueta,
whose antics parody those of their masters and invest the main
action with an air of farce.

The only significant emotional aspect of the myth that Rojas
retains is Medea's overpowering love for Jason, a love which
leads her to commit the most hideous crimes in behalf of her
husband but which, when rejected, turns to hate and a thirst for
vengeance. From this point on, she is no longer a human being,
nor is she troubled by opposing emotions. She loses no time in
slitting her children's throats ("por ser de Jasón reliquias");
she wastes not a tear in remorse. Thus, what was Medea's great
conflict in Euripides and Seneca, and even in Ovid's non-dramatic

version—maternal love versus desire for revenge—becomes in Rojas only one more unlovely act of a woman scorned.

Those who look upon Rojas as the Spanish Euripides cannot help feeling defrauded because he refused to approach Medea seriously.

Lucrecia y Tarquino

Because of its rarity, Rojas' *Lucrecia y Tarquino* has long escaped the attention of specialists in Spanish drama,[15] although it offers a remarkable example of baroque dramaturgy applied to a tragic tale of classical history. It also serves as a rejoinder to critics who have contended that Spanish dramatists of the Golden Age could not, or would not, address themselves to secular tragedy with universal themes.

The story of Lucrecia was a familiar one to Rojas' contemporaries because it was included in some of the most popular histories of Rome, readily available in translation, and because it was retold by medieval and Renaissance champions of women who looked upon the Roman matron as the very epitome of womanly virtue.[16] The source of Rojas' tragedy, however, was not one of the classical works (Dionysius of Halicarnassus, *The Roman Antiquities*, Titus Livy, *The History of Rome*, Ovid's *Fasti*, all of which contain the story); rather, the dramatist followed closely Francisco Bolle Pintaflor's Spanish translation, entitled *Tarquino el Soberbio* and printed in Madrid in 1635, of an Italian work, *Tarquino Superbo*, by Virgilio Malvezzi. The Marquis Malvezzi, an Italian diplomat in the service of Philip IV and a frequent visitor to the Spanish court in Rojas' day, has been called by Croce "the Seneca of the Italian language."[17] It is not surprising, therefore, that Rojas' tragedy (which incorporates versifications of long passages of Malvezzi's text) contains a large measure of Senecan stoicism.

Because of the fact that the story of Lucrecia was familiar to his audience, Rojas deliberately sought to create tension by obscuring and deferring the main conflict between Sexto Tarquino and Lucrecia, who do not meet until the final scene of the second act. However, the climate and mood of inevitable tragedy are early established by means of portentous symbolism, poetic imagery of ruin and destruction, and sharp contrasts of unevenly matched characters. The principal characters, all introduced in Act I, are: Tarquino el Soberbio, the tyrannical conqueror of Rome whose political philosophy anticipates the Machiavellian adage that it is better for a ruler to be feared than loved; Sexto Tarquino, his irascible son who has distinguished himself in the capture of Rome by his violence and cruelty; Colatino, Tarquino's general and Lucrecia's husband whose compassionate nature leads him to object to the treatment of the subjugated Romans, although he continues in Tarquino's service; Bruto, a Roman captive whose pretended madness permits him to make candid remarks about the fools and tyrants around him (he serves as the author's spokesman); Fabio, the *gracioso*; and Lucrecia, who, as the embodiment of Senecan stoicism, prizes only virtue.

Lucrecia's stoic creed is brought out in her first scene with her husband who has come to take leave of her. A wounded dove pierced by an arrow falls at Colatino's feet. Visibly shaken by this omen, he rages at the unseen hunter who shot the dove. Lucrecia's response, as she attempts to dispel her husband's fears, is charged with dramatic irony as she extols the dove, symbol of purity and of herself. Part of her speech and an English paraphrase follow:

> *Si el hado fatal permite*
> *que el pecho casto derrame*
> *líquido rubí inocente,*
> *esa inocencia le basta.*
> *¿Qué vida como una muerte,*
> *si lastimosa, inculpable,*
> *cuya piedad hace hermoso*
> *el más sangriento cadáver?* . . .
> *Muera el casto pecho al hierro*
> *antes que a la ofensa, y antes*
> *que ocasione pensamientos*
> *que injustamente le infamen.*
>
> (Act I, vv. 571 ff.)

[44]

(If fate permits the chaste breast to shed its innocent ruby-red blood, its very innocence will be compensation enough. What life can equal a death which, although lamentable, is blameless, and whose piety makes the bloodiest corpse beautiful? . . . Let the chaste breast die by the sword rather than by an offense to honor, and before it causes thoughts that may unjustly defame it.)

Lucrecia, like Seneca, has only contempt for death and fortune, because virtue and honor are the only good.[18] And later she has the opportunity to test her stoic convictions when, ironically, her husband's pride in her virtue forces her to abandon her cherished seclusion.

In Act II Sexto Tarquino summons a musician who sings of Dido's devotion to her deceased husband. Taking issue with Sexto's remark on the matchless fidelity of Dido, Colatino provokes a debate with Tarquino's other sons on the merits of their respective wives. Although Bruto warns Colatino of the tragic consequences that could result from such a debate, he, blinded by pride in Lucrecia, welcomes the proposal of a contest among the women. Returning to Rome, the other husbands are chagrined to find their wives making merry at a court festival. As part of the entertainment a skit is presented in which one of the courtiers, acting the part of Paris, is commissioned by Jupiter to hold a contest among the goddesses Venus, Pallas and Juno. As in the mythological contest, a golden apple is to be awarded to the fairest. Fabio's remarks on the physical defects of the goddesses parody the praise lavished by Colatino and the others on their wives. This comic interlude which divides the play symmetrically into two parts—preparation and resolution—heightens by contrast the seriousness of the contest to which Colatino has so foolishly committed his wife.

Proceeding to Colatino's home, the men find Lucrecia lamenting her husband's absence. Impressed by her beauty and virtue, Sexto Tarquino awards her the victory. The prince becomes so infatuated with her that he breaks a refreshment glass she has given him, another omen of her impending disaster. In dramatizing Sexto's infatuation with Lucrecia and his determination to possess her, Rojas follows Malvezzi's lead in showing that his "lust was occasioned as much by the chastity of Lucrecia as by her beauty." Malvezzi goes on to explain (as translated by the Earl of Monmouth):

Men lustfully given, cause all their senses, yea, the understanding itselfe to minister provocations for the satisfying of that sense: beauty, birth, sweet odours, harmony, all which have nothing to doe with feeling; and which is worse, Vertue herselfe, and amongst vertues, very Chastity, the very opposite to Lust, does more incite thereunto: Vertue is so lovely, that shee makes herselfe bee loved, yea, even by Vice . . .[19]

The reason, of course, for Rojas' insistence upon Lucrecia's virtue as a chief cause in provoking Sexto Tarquino's lust is that it heightens the irony of her tragic fate.

In Act III, during Colatino's absence, Sexto Tarquino gains admission into Lucrecia's home under the pretense that his coach broke down. He soon declares his love, but she rejects him, retiring for the night. While Colatino, musing upon the omen of the wounded dove, is returning home, the rape is consummated. Sexto Tarquino himself relates the circumstances: he awakened Lucrecia and threatened to kill her with a knife if she did not submit to him. She fainted and he ravished her unconscious body. It is worthy of note that Rojas differs from Malvezzi and other authors in presenting these circumstances. In all other works Sextus Tarquin threatens to kill Lucrecia and one of her slaves whom, he would claim, he found in adulterous relations. Lucrecia submits to him because she cannot bear the thought of the calumny.

Rojas and Shakespeare are the only two writers who make any effort to portray the feelings of guilt and remorse which prey upon the rapist. In Malvezzi, "Tarquin leaves as happy as he is triumphant"; but in Shakespeare's poem, as in Rojas' play, "He runs, and chides his vanish'd, loathed delight." (*The Rape of Lucrece*, v. 742)

When her friends and relatives are gathered in her house (which, symbolically, is in utter darkness), Lucrecia laments the catastrophe that has befallen her, insisting that she was a faultless victim. Then, pondering the cause of her tragedy, she perceives that her virtue, her *honestidad,* was responsible for her undoing:

[46]

> ¿Pero, quién pudo alentar   **17**
> aquel sacrílego monstruo
> a tanta maldad? ¿Fue acaso
> mi honestidad? ¿Cómo, cómo
> el más pernicioso vicio
> halló en la virtud apoyo?
> (Act III, vv. 2120 ff.)

> (But what could have incited
> that sacrilegious monster
> to such evil? Was it perhaps
> my chastity? How, oh how
> could the most pernicious vice
> find an ally in virtue?)

It is no wonder that Lucrecia's recognition is put in the form of a question. One always remains somewhat incredulous on discovering the truth of a paradox.

Finally, rather than ask her family to take revenge, Lucrecia refuses to permit her would-be avengers to become involved in a blood-feud, preferring "to take vengeance upon herself" by committing suicide. Wisely Rojas did not extend the action of the play beyond Lucrecia's death. Wisely he did not clutter up the conclusion with scenes designed to gratify the spectators' sense of outraged justice by showing Sexto Tarquino getting his deserts. There is only the promise that retribution will be had.

Lucrecia is one of the very few tragic protagonists of the Golden Age who can point to virtue as the cause of her demise. Despite her merits, however, she is not a wholly convincing tragic character. It was for no idle reason that Aristotle observed that the proper tragic hero is "a man who is not eminently good and just, yet whose misfortune is brought about not by vice or depravity, but by some error or frailty." [20] The fact is that Lucrecia is simply too eminently good, resembling a martyr in a saint's play more than a figure in a human tragedy. It is interesting to conjecture whether Shakespeare, who portrayed at times some nearly faultless characters—Desdemona, Cordelia, Edgar—but who generally created figures made of less flawless stuff, did not perceive the difficulties of making Lucrecia a tragic protagonist and chose instead to make her the subject of a poem.

More convincing than Lucrecia is Colatino, who is the agent of his wife's tragedy and his own misfortune, because recognition, despite many warnings, comes to him too late. Colatino's pride in Lucrecia is understandable, but his tragic fault, like that of Oedipus and King Lear, is a lack of perception. He is probably Rojas' most Aristotelian hero.

Progne y Filomena

One of the best Spanish plays based on a mythological theme and one of Rojas' most impressive tragedies, *Progne y Filomena* was performed in the Royal Palace on January 10, 1636. It was one of the most widely performed of his plays in the seventeenth century and one which was often reprinted in the eighteenth. It was also recast by Tomás Sebastián y Latre, whose *refundición* went through two printings (Zaragoza, 1772; Madrid, 1773) but failed to capture, despite its neo-classical regularity, the compelling intensity of the original. It is also one of Rojas' plays that has provoked considerable critical discussion because of its unusual treatment of the Spanish honor code and because of its controversial comic subplot.

The sources of Rojas' tragedy are two: the story of Tereus, Procne and Philomela related in Book VI of Ovid's *Metamorphoses*, and Guillén de Castro's *Progne y Filomena*, printed in 1618 in the *Primera parte* of his plays. Ovid's treatment of the myth was, of course, the source of the many revenge tragedies written in other European countries in the sixteenth and seventeenth centuries on the two sisters—Philomela, the victim of Tereus' lust, and Procne, the offended wife, who vied with Medea for popularity as female revengers.

In general, Guillén de Castro followed Ovid rather closely, but he added several incidents of his own invention, some of which Rojas borrowed. In particular, Castro created Teosindo, brother of King Tereo, who comes to Athens to arrange Tereo's marriage to one of the daughters of King Pandión. After Teosindo sends portraits of Progne and Filomena to his brother, Tereo chooses Progne to be his bride. The play opens with a scene in which Filomena expresses her grief because Teosindo, with whom she is in love, will return to Thrace immediately after the wedding. Upon his arrival, Tereo is smitten by the beauty of Filomena, but he is dismayed to learn that the portraits were mislabelled and that he is to marry Progne. Tereo's suspicion that Teosindo has deceived him grows when his brother blames the error on the artist and later confesses that he is in love with Filomena. Tereo conceals his dissatisfaction with Progne, but resolves to possess Filomena at any cost. Teosindo and Filomena play into his hands when, in order to avoid being separated, they secure Pandión's permission for her to accompany Progne on an extended visit to Thrace.

These incidents, with a few modifications, are incorporated in the first act of Rojas' play. Although Filomena is engaged to marry an Albanian prince, she is secretly in love with Tereo's brother (named Hipólito rather than Teosindo) to whom she has surrendered her virginity. It is intimated that Hipólito duped his brother into marrying Progne, and the lovers deceive both Progne and King Pandrón (instead of Pandión) into believing that Filomena cannot bear being separated from her sister. In short, the love of Hipólito and Filomena is attended by moral guilt and a series of deceptions of the kind which almost always bring about some measure of retribution in Golden Age drama. Thus, Rojas attempts to show much more than Castro that Filomena is partially responsible for the calamity which befalls her.

Apart from the romantic incidents with which Guillén de Castro and Rojas fill out the first act of their tragedies, both dramatists follow Ovid closely in portraying Tereo as a passionate man who cannot resist his desire for Filomena. In Rojas' play, however, Tereo is not presented as a wanton villain but as a man of conscience who restrains for two years his passion to possess her. Then, learning that she intends to flee with Hipólito, Tereo, acting out of a desire for revenge as well as lust, carries out the rape of Filomena with chilling resoluteness. He also cuts her tongue so that she cannot divulge the crime.

But all is not done with Tereo. Goaded by his conscience, he berates himself for neglecting his loving wife and for continuing to lust after Filomena after he has raped her:

¡Que conociendo mi mal
No sepa yo remediarle!
[Este amor] ya no es llama de mi fuego,
Rebeldía es de mi sangre!
                    (*BAE,* III, 53c)

(To think that knowing the cause of my malady
I do not know how to remedy it!
This love is no longer a flame of my fire,
It is a rebellion of my blood!)

Indeed, Tereo's abiding passion for Filomena is a "rebellion of the blood"—and a true tragic weakness. Tereo resembles Phaedra (and certain of Euripides' other characters) whose dark blood, overcoming reason and conscience, leads them to destroy their lives.

It is in the manner that Progne and Filomena exact vengeance on Tereo that Rojas differs most from Ovid and Guillén de Castro. In Ovid's treatment, the sisters' revenge is similar to that of Atreus in Seneca's *Thyestes*. Procne butchers her son by Tereus, serving his flesh and blood to her unsuspecting husband. And,

> High in the chair
> sat Tereus, proud, and feasting, almost greedy
> On the flesh of his own flesh, and in his darkness
> Of mind, he calls: "Bring Itys here!" and Procne
> Cannot conceal her cruel joy; she is eager
> To be the herald of her bloody murder.
> "He has come in," she answers, and he looks
> Around, asks where the boy is, asks again,
> Keeps calling, and Philomela, with hair all bloody,
> Springs at him, and hurls the bloody head of Itys
> Full in his father's face.
> (*Metamorphoses,* tr. Rolfe Humphries, Book VI, vv. 648-58.)

As Ovid concludes the myth, the sisters elude Tereus' sword when they are transformed into birds, and "Tereus, swift in grief and lust for vengeance,/Himself becomes a bird . . ."

In Guillén de Castro's play, Pandión's daughters exact the same revenge. The unpredictable Valencian dramatist, however,

[50]

salvages a happy ending. Chastened by their suffering and bloody excesses, Tereo and Progne are reconciled. All characters, except poor Itis (Itys), look forward to a bright future.

Rojas' treatment of the sisters' revenge has attracted attention because it has been regarded as involving an original and daring departure from the Spanish honor code (the requirements of which were often forced upon mythological characters who found their way into Spanish plays). Rojas' women are seldom content to let their men redress wrongs done to them; they must draw the blood of their offenders themselves. It is not surprising, then, that Progne and Filomena quarrel with one another as to who should have priority in taking revenge on Tereo. Rojas' originality does not consist so much in having the women avenge themselves—the same thing happens in his sources—but rather in that Progne feels that she has the right and even the duty under the honor code to castigate her husband's adultery. As it turns out, however, the sisters compromise, joining together to riddle Tereo's body. The audience is then treated to a view of the corpse in the blood-spattered bed.

Interspersed throughout the main action is a comic subplot involving Juanete and Chilindrón, who are not conventional *graciosos* in that they are not in the service of the principal characters. Rather, they are unattached menials whose chief mission is to make life miserable for each other. Many of Rojas' plays have been criticized for their extensive comic intrusions but none has been more generally anathematized than *Progne y Filomena*. Critics of all persuasions have taken turns during the last two centuries in condemning its comic subplot for its irrelevance and lack of taste. The fact is, as I have tried to demonstrate elsewhere, that the subplot has considerable relevance in that it often linked with the main plot and it, too, has revenge at its crux.[21] But the type of revenge dealt out by Juanete and Chilindrón to each other is hardly consonant with the gory business of revenge tragedy. One example should suffice.

In order to get even with his rival, Chilindrón, knowing that Juanete has an inordinate sweet tooth, leaves a jar of preserves filled with a purgative where he will find it. As is to be expected Juanete finds the preserves and bolts them down. The purgative takes effect, causing Juanete to writhe in pain during one of the most crucial moments of the play (as Tereo searches the forest for Filomena immediately prior to the rape). Tragedy may well profit from well-timed comic relief, but the relief here is out of place. Tragedy seeks another kind of catharsis.

It is significant, perhaps, that those who have protested loudest about the comic intrusions in *Progne y Filomena* have also admitted the overall excellence of the play.[22] Its skillfully structured plot, its exquisite poetry, its convincing characterization make it one of Rojas' most unforgettable plays.

II *The Revenge Tragedy*

Morir pensando matar is one of the few revenge tragedies written in seventeenth-century Spain, as distinguished from the Spanish honor dramas in which, of course, revenge is an important element. The two types of plays may be more closely related than has been realized, however, and a systematic study of their relationship needs to be made. The revenge tragedy, as it was cultivated throughout Europe in the late Renaissance, has its origins in those of Seneca's tragedies which have blood-revenge as the dominant motive, namely, *Thyestes, Medea,* and *Agamemnon.* Revenge is not limited to honor offenses but is based on the *lex talionis,* that unlovely rule which, rather than exhorting men to turn the other cheek, bids them to exact an eye for an eye.

Neo-Senecan dramatists of the sixteenth century not only equalled or exceeded their master in the cult of bloody vengeance but spiced their compositions with a variety of appalling atrocities. They peopled their plays with perverse psychopaths whose only concern seemed to be to make life hell on earth for everybody else. They invented new horrors and refined old tortures. They dismembered the living and piled up corpses on the stage for the delectation of the audience. While Spanish dramatists seldom went as far as their Italian and English contemporaries in cramming multiple murders and physical horrors into a single play (Thomas Kyd's *The Spanish Tragedy,* 1587–1589, contains no fewer than ten violent deaths), Juan de la Cueva (1550–1610), Cristóbal de Virués (1550–1609?), and Lupercio Leonardo de Argensola (1559–1613), among others, wrote chilling dramas in the Senecan tradition. Blood-revenge was their common denominator.

Morir pensando matar

The plot of *Morir pensando matar* is based on the story of King Alboin and Rosamund, a favorite subject of neo-Senecan dramatists everywhere.[23] The ultimate source of Rojas' play is Paulus Diaconus, *Historia Langobardorum* (c. 790), which contains the definitive form of the legend. Rojas, however, probably became acquainted with it through its inclusion in Pero Mexía's *Silva de varia lección* (Seville, 1540), where it is related in Chapter XXIV of Book III.[24] The dramatist was also familiar with Gabriel Lasso de la Vega's ballad, "Romance Dezimoséptimo, de la sangrienta vengança de Rosimunda con Alboino su marido Rey de los Longobardos," which in turn is based on Pero Mexía's prose account.[25] In general Rojas followed the broad outline of the legend rather closely, but he changed the names of some characters, added others, and invented several episodes, especially those having to do with the counter-revenge taken against Rosimunda after Alboino's murder. Here is a résumé of the plot.

Flabio, the Duke of Verona, relates to his fiancée Albisinda, sister of King Alboino of the Lombards, her brother's victory over Floribundo, king of the Gepids. Not only was the latter killed in the battle but his daughter Rosimunda was forced to marry his conqueror. Later, at a banquet held to celebrate his victory, Alboino offends his bride by offering a toast from the skull of her dead father. Not convinced that this custom of the Lombards was indeed a tribute to the vanquished (as it was supposed to be), Rosimunda swears to take revenge on her husband. She elicits the aid of Duke Leoncio, who is in love with her.

Taking advantage of the darkness to pretend that she is Albisinda, Rosimunda asks Flabio to kill Alboino on the grounds that he opposes "their" marriage. Shocked by the request, Flabio goes to warn Alboino. Meanwhile the king is disturbed by premonitions of death, premonitions which do not leave him when Leoncio reports that Rosimunda, now pacified, is coming to see him. When Alboino falls asleep, Rosimunda ties him in his chair, and Leoncio kills him with Flabio's dagger. Flabio is imprisoned for the murder.

Addressing the crowd that has gathered for Rosimunda's and Leoncio's coronation, Albisinda denounces the couple as murderers and traitors. She and her followers liberate Flabio, then go to seize the tyrants. In the royal palace Leoncio becomes unnerved when he stumbles on a portrait of Alboino that has fallen from the wall. Rosimunda orders a glass of water for him, but after drinking half of it, he suspects that it is poison and forces her to drink the rest. Indeed it is the poison that he had prepared for Flabio and that a servant brought to him by mistake. When Albisinda and Flabio arrive, their followers want to use their swords to hasten the deaths of the culprits, but Flabio restrains them, preferring that they die of the poison administered by their own hands. It is worthy of note that Flabio, as a morally scrupulous character, avoids the temptation into which most counter-revengers fall, the temptation to take vengeance into his own hands rather than let Heaven punish the evildoers in its own way.

True to its type, *Morir pensando matar* contains most of the standard elements of revenge tragedy. Its action is distributed in three stages corresponding to the three acts: the events leading up to Rosimunda's resolution to take blood-revenge on her father's offender, revenge which is binding on her as a dutiful daughter (Act I); the machinations of the revenger and her accomplice (who, as in most revenge tragedies, are involved in adultery) to bring about the death of the offender (Act II); the counter-revenge taken by the family and friends of the victim, with the consequent death of the revenger and her accomplice (Act III). The structure of the plot, like that of most revenge tragedies, is of the type that one of Rojas' contemporaries called *de doble constitución,* "in which, with great clarity, two different and sorrowful events are introduced and which, recurring throughout the whole of the tragedy, form and compose it." [26]

The play also contains the rather stereotyped characterization and many of the devices found in most revenge tragedies.

Rosimunda, in her role as the revenger, is a sympathetic character at the beginning of the play, one who is "much more sinned against than sinning." Faithful to the memory of her father, she is naturally incensed when her barbaric husband uses his skull for a drinking vessel. As is customary in the genre, she pronounces a lengthy elegy in praise of the deceased king, and, equally typical, utters a curse upon his offender: "May your best friend kill you/ after having dishonored you." (vv. 585–86) The curse is later realized when Duke Leoncio, Alboino's "best friend," usurps his marital bed, then kills him. But if revenge is a sacred duty for Rosimunda, she soon loses all sense of justice and resorts to criminal acts against the innocent to further her ends. Thus converted into a Machiavellian intriguer, she becomes—as most revengers inevitably do—the villain of the play.

A common device found in many revenge tragedies is to have a character, marked for death, read about the demise of an historical figure whose fate anticipates his own. It occurs in Rojas' play when Alboino, who has already had premonitions of death, learns that Rosimunda is coming to visit him. To while away the time he picks up a volume of Suetonius' *Lives of the Caesars,* opening it at random to the account of Agrippina's murder of her husband, Claudius. This bedtime reading does not assuage Alboino's anxiety, and he has every reason to be alarmed: he will soon die at the hands of his own vengeful wife and her paramour.

The trouble with most revengers and counter-revengers (if we can deduce a moral lesson common to these plays) is that they never know when to stop. Their grievances are often real enough and cry out for justice, but revenge continues to beget revenge until innocent bystanders are caught up in the bloody feud. All, revengers and counter-revengers alike, are usually guilty of violating the biblical injunction, "Vengeance is mine, saith the Lord." To be sure, Rosimunda calls upon Heaven to avenge her, but impatient with the slowness of divine justice, she takes revenge in her own hands. But Heaven, as in most of these plays, does not let murder go unatoned; and so it is that Rosimunda and her accomplice die accidentally—and providentially—from the poison they intended for others. In her final speech Rosimunda recognizes that Heaven willed her punishment. Flabio, as we have already seen, is different from most counter-revengers in that he is unwilling to interfere with divine justice by hastening the death of the tyrants.

Morir pensando matar is not one of Rojas' most poetic plays, but some measure of his skill as poet and dramatist can be gathered by comparing it with Manuel Morchón's *La razón busca venganza* (Madrid, 1657), a later play also based on Pero Mexía's account of the legend.

III   The Cain and Abel Plays

Rojas' three tragedies involving father-son conflicts (*No hay ser padre siendo rey, El Caín de Cataluña* and *El más impropio verdugo por la más justa venganza*) can properly be called Cain and Abel plays because, in addition to involving the "conflict between generations," all are related to the story of the biblical brothers. Also all three plays contain similarities in plot and characterization, although they differ in their dénouements. In each, an aging father has two sons, one a violent wretch who hates his father and harbors monstrous envy toward his brother—in short, a personification of Evil; the other, a model of filial obedience and altruism—the symbol of Good. Pitted against each other as rivals in love, the wicked brother murders or intends to murder his virtuous brother, whereupon the father (as king or ruler in two of the plays) is called upon to sit in judgment upon his criminal son. Will he mete out justice to him or will he spare his life? Such is the father's dilemma, a horrible moral dilemma. Obviously the drift of these plays—in pattern of incident, conflict, and the antithesis of characters—smacks of melodrama. It is worth noting, too, that the villainous brothers are highly reminiscent of the raging, bloody tyrants of Senecan drama.

No hay ser padre siendo rey

The source of *No hay ser padre siendo rey,* performed on January 1, 1635, is Guillén de Castro's *La justicia en la piedad.* However, unlike Castro's Carlos, who is a fiend with no redeeming qualities, Rojas' Rugero is a man whose errors are owed to his "tragic flaw." The fact is, though, that his flaw—his overweening arrogance—is one that does not permit him easily to be distinguished from the most ruthless villains.

After enumerating the long list of crimes imputed to his son Rugero, the king of Poland demands that he mend his ways and especially that he become reconciled with his brother, Alejandro, whom he had threatened to kill. Ostensibly Rugero seeks a reconciliation with Alejandro only because his father ordered it, but in an aside he lets it be known that he really loves his brother but cannot express his affection because of his own arrogant nature.

But if Rugero's bark is worse than his bite for his brother, this is not so for others who stand in his way. In love with Casandra, whom he intends to possess by force if necessary, he goes to her home where he finds her in bed with a man whom he believes to be the Duke Federico. Not knowing that Alejandro is secretly married to Casandra, he mistakenly kills him. Rugero is made to realize the enormity of his crime when he emerges from the scene of the murder and encounters his own ghost (shades of Seneca!) who leaves him dazed and wounded.

Later, imprisoned by his father, who intends to make of him an example of kingly justice, Rugero laments the death of his brother and regrets that he has acquired self-knowledge too late. His only defense is that he had not intended to kill his brother; he erred in his victim. Now that the prince is repentant, it is not surprising to find that the king, in response to the demands of a public uprising that the life of the heir be spared, abdicates the throne in favor of his son. Such was the solution Rojas found in Guillén de Castro's play and so he left it. The conclusion is also somewhat similar to that of Calderón's *La vida es sueño* in that Rugero, like Segismundo, presumably proves his fitness to rule by overcoming his passions and dominating himself.

El Caín de Cataluña

Indebted in part to Guillén de Castro's *La justicia en la piedad* but more to his own *No hay ser padre siendo rey, El Caín de*

Cataluña (of uncertain date) shows Rojas' continued preoccupation with the problems of evil and with fraternal and filial conflicts. Apparently not satisfied with the characterization of Rugero nor with the solution he gave to the earlier play, he employs the same basic situation in *El Caín* but concentrates his attention on the protagonist. The result is one of the ugliest human beings ever to cross the Spanish stage.

Berenguel, second son of the Count of Barcelona, is a savage sadist whose misanthropy is boundless. The cold enemas, the beatings, the brutalities he orders inflicted on inferiors are bad enough, but his envy of his brother, Ramón, is satanic. Berenguel envies his brother's every possession: his horse, his sword, his clothes, and, rather pathetically, his verses. Nor is Berenguel's envy limited to matters of social prestige. It is omnifarious. Not content with having been given Ramón's first fiancée (he threatened to burn down the city if he could not have her), he covets his second fiancée, determining to have her at any cost.

Learning that his brother is returning in triumph from a campaign against the Turks (another bitter pill for him to swallow), Berenguel decides to murder him when he disembarks. He does. For a brief moment he is overcome with remorse, as desolate as the biblical Cain trembling before divine justice, but his remorse soon gives way to fear for his misshapen ego.

Later, imprisoned by his father, Berenguel disclaims any responsibility for being his brother's keeper; and when Ramón's ghost appears to him, his only regret is that he cannot restore him to life in order to kill him again. Finally, after Berenguel has been sentenced to death by the Council of State, the Count, in his capacity as ruler, signs the death warrant, but acting as a father, he aids him in escaping from prison. Berenguel reverts to the blackguard he has always been—a gouging, cursing wretch who swears vengeance on his father for his last paternal act. His evil spirit is silenced by a sentinel's bullet (anachronistically, since the murder took place historically in 1082) as he scales the prison wall.

Berenguel is certainly no Aristotelian tragic hero. He is an utter villain whose downfall is brought about not by error or frailty but through depravity. Though he is related through perversity to Shakespeare's Richard III, he has neither his physical courage nor his fiendish cunning. He does not even have Richard's ambition to give shading to his blackness. Nevertheless, he is not exceeded by Richard or Edmund in *King Lear* in his awesome dedication to evil, and he probably surpasses them both in hideous envy. Berenguel remains the archrepresentative of what Unamuno called "a genuinely Spanish capital sin . . . envy." [27]

El más impropio verdugo por la más justa venganza

While Berenguel is reminiscent of the Senecan tyrant in his perversity and crude loudness, even more tumultuous is Alejandro in *El más impropio verdugo por la más justa venganza* (first performed on February 14, 1637). Recognizing, like Don Juan Tenorio, no law but his own will, Alejandro is a forthright savage who, despite his homicidal tendencies, retains a certain grandeur. Failing in his attempt to rape Leonor, whose home he entered by breaking into an adjoining convent, he encounters his brother (Diana's sweetheart) in the dark. Questioned about his identity, Alejandro identifies himself as a "devil so mad and arrogant that he does not flee from crosses or calvaries." (*BAE*, I, 169b) Recognizing his brother after injuring him in swordplay, Alejandro would like to cut his heart out because, as he says, he is a second Cain, the Cain of Florence.

Although a Ghibelline, Alejandro does not let political affiliation stand in the way of his ambition—to hack the streets of Florence clean of men. Guelphs and Ghibellines alike fall before his sword. Fortunately, before he has depopulated the city, Alejandro and the male members of his family (who comprehend the exigencies of the honor code although Florentine officials do not) are imprisoned and sentenced to death for an honor slaying. When no executioner can be found, Alejandro offers his services, exulting in the prospect of killing his father and brother on the public scaffold. When César Salviati tries to reason with his son, Alejandro makes clear why he hates him: "Isn't it enough that you are my father?" (*BAE*, II, 186b) Not only does Alejandro see his father as a symbol of authority who imposes restraint upon his vital urges, but he looks on him as a natural enemy. Also, because he finds himself difficult to live with, he volunteered to execute his father, "To punish you for having given me my being." (*BAE*, III, 187c)

Unable to move his son, Salviati contrives to beat him out of the role of executioner. Only thus is the libido of this self-styled "toro español agarrochado" put to rest. Moments later Salviati, with bloody knife in hand, descends the scaffold saying that he has killed "a son more wicked than any recorded in antiquity." (*BAE*, III, 189c) Again, as in *Progne y Filomena*, the audience is treated to a view of the corpse. Salviati and the chaste Carlos go free.

Perhaps it is vain to try to redeem Alejandro from the ranks of the criminally insane, but one can at least perceive the compulsions which made him become the self-appointed blood-letter of Florence. He can be "explained" by considering the age in which he was born. Out of the vast and often confusing literature written about the Baroque during the past three decades, near unanimity emerges on one point: in Spain where the Counter-Reformation made itself most strongly felt, man, still savoring the delights and freedom unloosed by the Renaissance, ran afoul of the new order. He emerged an ambivalent creature, torn between the desire for self-assertion and the fear of not conforming to norms imposed upon him from without. He generally acquiesced—thus the considerable number of half-baked rebels whose little revolts never quite come off. But this is not true of Alejandro. He goes down fighting for self-assertion and hurling defiance at all authority, human and divine.

Along with its preoccupation with the Baroque, modern criticism has been equally entertained by the chase of the Oedipus complex, and a thorough beating of literary bushes has produced a lot of game. Segismundo in Calderón's *La vida es sueño* emerges as an embryonic Oedipus who never goes beyond the stage of threatening his father.[28] Hamlet, more complicated if not more "profound" than Segismundo, turns out to suffer from the same complex, but for him the father image appears "split in two— the father loved and revered, and the hated tyrannical usurper."[29] In Rojas we need not look for anything so subtle. His ungrateful sons chide their fathers for begetting them for their own pleasure. They do not attempt to conceal their hostility. Alejandro is but the ultimate and most forthright in manifesting his parricidal urges. He is Rojas' most Freudian creation and one of the great rebels born of the Baroque.

IV   The Tragedies of National History

The Numantia Plays

Numancia cercada and *Numancia destruída* are of interest for a number of reasons. They constitute Rojas' only extant two-part play, and although the date of their composition is not known, there is slight evidence to suggest that they were written early in his career. Both figure in the repertory of an unidentified theatrical company, a repertory consisting of twenty-six plays, none of which, insofar as it is known, was written after 1630.[30] They are also among the few historical plays that Rojas ever wrote, and if one excludes *El Caín de Cataluña* (which is based on an historical episode but whose concern is not historical), they are his only tragedies based on national history. Both plays are indebted to Cervantes' *La Numancia,* providing an opportunity to compare how the two dramatists, writing some fifty years apart, went about dramatizing the fall of the Iberian city.[31]

Cervantes' tragedy was written two or three years after his return to Spain in 1580 from captivity in Algiers. Although it has been criticized as being more epical than dramatic and for having an episodic plot, it is a moving play, notable for its patriotic fervor and its noble sentiment. The first of its four acts begins with the arrival of Escipión (Emiliano) to take command of the Roman siege of Numantia, which has resisted the invaders for more than sixteen years. After initiating reforms in the Roman army, Escipión makes known to his officers his plan to starve the city into submission. The allegorical figure of the River *Duero* appears to prophesy that although *España* will be defeated on this occasion, she will rise to greatness in the future under Philip II.

Most of the action of the remaining acts takes place in the city itself where the Numantians offer sacrifices, attended by unfavorable omens. When a resuscitated corpse prophesies that Numantia will perish by its own hand, the sorcerer Marquino, in a startling scene, commits suicide by leaping into the open grave. Teógenes, leader of the Numantians, then orders his people to destroy their possessions and themselves by fire in order to thwart the Romans. The allegorical figures War, Sickness, and Hunger appear to comment on the horrifying events taking place in the city. When Escipión and his followers enter the razed city, they find alive only the boy Bariato, who has taken refuge in a tower. Escipión promises to reward him if he surrenders, but the boy plunges to his death. The Roman leader applauds the heroism of the boy and the city, but remains dejected over his empty victory. Fame, dressed in white, enters to pronounce the final speech extolling the bravery of Numantia whose memory will endure forever.

One of Cervantes' major concerns was to show the suffering and heroism of a beleaguered people. For this purpose he employs more than sixty characters, many of whom are nameless but representative Numantians, Women, and Children. While he invented the episode of Marandro and Lira to portray the devotion and generosity of young lovers victimized by adversity, none of his characters exists independently of the war that blights their lives. There are no comic elements in the play. La Numancia is in every sense a collective tragedy.[32]

Rojas retained virtually all the historical events dramatized in Cervantes' tragedy, and he added several others (the arrival of King Jugurta with Numidian troops, etc.).[33] He also retained the legendary episode of the boy who leaps to his death from the tower, an episode which is more similar in detail than any other which the plays have in common. The use of allegorical characters was suggested to Rojas by Cervantes' tragedy, although he changed their names and roles to suit his own aims. However, it is in the dramatization of non-historical episodes that the plays differ most.

Of the thirty-odd characters in Rojas' two-part play, only three have names identical with those in Cervantes' tragedy: Escipión (or Cipión), Jugurta, and Cayo Mario, although the latter two have only minor roles in La Numancia. Rojas' Retógenes corresponds to Teógenes, although historically Retógenes Caravino and Teógenes were different persons. The relationship of Retógenes and Florinda, first as sweethearts, then as husband and wife, has little resemblance, however, to that of Teógenes and his unnamed wife. Rather, Rojas' couple is more similar to Cervantes' Marandro and Lira; and curiously, too, Rojas' peasant husband and wife, Tronco and Olalla, were also suggested by Cervantes' sweethearts, whose roles they parody. One of the most pathetic scenes in Cervantes' *Numantia* occurs when Marandro returns from his foray into the Roman camp with blood-smeared bread for Lira, then dies at her feet. In *Numancia destruída* Tronco returns with a piece of bread from the Roman camp to his starving wife, but he refuses to share it with her, arguing that since she abides in him, he feeds her by feeding himself. Certainly no one would be more surprised than Cervantes to find his tender lovers converted into an abusive couple whose role is to provide such bizarre humor.

Whereas Cervantes' tragedy can be described as a vast canvas of war in which the figures are not merely foreshortened but more or less uniformly dwarfed, Rojas' two-part play is dominated by human subjects who often obscure the background of war and exist independently of it. All are bound by personal ties which have nothing to do with the war, or for which the war is at best a pretext, as may be seen in the various romantic subplots involving all the principal characters on both sides in amorous intrigue. Even Cipión, the tragic antagonist, becomes involved in the romantic subplots when he advises Artemisa, who has come from Numidia in pursuit of King Jugurta who has lost his heart to Florinda, as to how she can regain her man. The fact is that Rojas' plays have two major actions, love and war. At times they are developed independently, at times simultaneously, and at times they are fused. It is the alternation and occasional fusion of the actions of love and war that give the plays their peculiar rhythm, making them so different from Cervantes' tragedy.

It is in the person of Retógenes that the actions of love and war achieve unity, and in large measure *Numancia cercada* and *Numancia destruída* are the personal tragedies of the Numantian leader. In the first play, when he quarrels with Megara over the love of Florinda and threatens to destroy the city if he cannot have her, Retógenes resembles the petulant lover of cape-and-sword drama much more than a tragic hero. The vicissitudes of the war follow the vagaries of his love, as fortune calls the tune, and the survival of the city seems to depend upon the love life of the Leading Man. In *Numancia destruída,* however, Retógenes begins to act more consistently like the Spanish Mars he is called in the play. In Act II, after the Numantians have successfully resisted a Roman attack, Cipión sends Jugurta to him to negotiate a truce. The Numantian leader now has an opportunity to end the war on honorable terms, but intoxicated with pride—pride in himself, pride in his people—he hopes for a decisive victory over the Romans.

Retógenes' ambition to overcome Rome leads directly to the city's fall, and Rojas borrowed from Cervantes the idea of the omens used to prepare for its demise. An eagle descends, placing a laurel crown on his head, an event which Retógenes interprets to mean that Numantia will be victorious over Rome; but the eagle returns and snatches the crown from him. Musing upon the significance of this omen, Retógenes falls asleep. In his dream *Olvido* (Oblivion) appears on-stage, flanked by *Roma* and *Numancia* who have their swords drawn. Their confrontation in this allegorical play-within-a-play (which occupies forty verses of octaves) concludes with *Numancia's* refusal to surrender and, in order to escape Oblivion, her consequent suicide.

Apart from the remarkable empathy of this scene in which the audience is made to share Retógenes' dream, it also marks the beginning of the dénouement and points to the conclusion. Like Oedipus who wished to take upon himself all the sufferings of Thebes occasioned by his unwitting errors, Retógenes, unable to help his starving people, addresses an apostrophe to Fortune in which he offers himself up as a sacrificial victim if his city is spared. Later, when only two or three Numantians remain, Retógenes, realizing that his own death is imminent, pronounces his final soliloquy. Although he is given several soliloquies in the two plays, his final one, addressed to the River Duero, marks one of Rojas' supreme efforts to create the lyricism proper to the cathartic process. It ends with this *lira:*

> *Dame, río sagrado,*
> *para templar mi fuego, claras linfas;*
> *en tu coro argentado*
> *estas desdichas cantarán tus ninfas*

con su divino acento,
si desdichas cantadas dan contento.
                    (Act III, folio 14v.)

(Give me, sacred river,
your clear water to temper my fire;
in your silvery chorus
your nymphs will sing of these misfortunes
with their divine accent,
if misfortunes, sung, give contentment.)

Rojas concerned himself with all of Cervantes' principal themes—war, hunger, and fame—but he subsumed them, in their finest expression, to the subjective preoccupations of Retógenes. So it is that the lyricism of Cervantes' Spain and Duero, choral characters in a collective tragedy, find their counterpart in the soliloquies—in the "desdichas cantadas"—of Retógenes. He is a baroque approximation of the classical tragic hero, and Rojas' Numantia plays are largely this hero's personal tragedy.

CHAPTER 4

The Honor Dramas

S EVERAL generations of critics have remarked on the origi
nality of Rojas' treatment of conjugal honor, an originality
which probably evolved, I would suggest, from his abiding in
terest in episodes of classical history and mythology in which
women assume the initiative in taking revenge on those who
offend them. This interest is readily apparent in his tragedies
in which women are cast in the role of avengers. Rosimunda in
Morir pensando matar plots the murder of her husband because
he offended her by insulting her deceased father. Medea avenges
herself on Jason by killing their children because he abandoned
her for another woman. Lucrecia kills herself because she be
lieves that she alone can properly remove the dishonor inflicted
upon her. And Progne and Filomena quarrel with one another
as to who should have priority in killing King Tereo, who was
unfaithful to the one and who raped the other. In a strange
reversal of the traditional position of women with regard to the
honor code, the two sisters are the first women in Spanish
drama to insist that they are privileged, even obliged, to inflic
the supreme penalty on their offender. It is not surprising
then, that Rojas' heroines in plays of contemporary setting should
have unusual notions about their prerogatives in matters in
volving conjugal honor.

In addition to his tragedies, many of Rojas' plays involve
women's honor but in only five of them does conjugal honor
form the crux. Only two, *Del rey abajo, ninguno* (if Rojas wrote
it) and *Casarse por vengarse*, are conventional honor dramas
in that the husband tries to kill his wife because she, whether a
fault or not, brings dishonor on him, in his own eyes, by attract
ing the improper attentions of another man. Three of Rojas'
plays, *Peligrar en los remedios, Cada cual lo que le toca*, and
La traición busca el castigo, are unconventional not only in that

the wife is spared in circumstances that might well lead to her death but, more important, either the husband or wife acts or speaks in a manner that calls into question the validity of the basic concepts of conjugal honor as they were customarily presented on the Spanish stage.

Whereas earlier critics commented summarily on Rojas' unusual treatment of conjugal honor, in his edition of *Cada cual lo que le toca* Américo Castro elaborates on the importance of married women in Rojas' theater and defines their relationship to the honor code. Castro concludes, "With respect to our play, it is fitting, of course, to affirm that if it does not present a theory of honor different from that which appears in the general run of our theatrical works, its dénouement totally subverts the usual principles of honor." [1] Castro then suggests that Rojas' pronounced feminism may be owed to the persistence of Erasmian ideas on the dignity of women which enjoyed a short-lived vogue in sixteenth-century Spain.[2]

We shall look at Rojas' unconventional honor dramas first, saving *Del rey abajo, ninguno* for the last.

I *Peligrar en los remedios*

Preserved in a partially autograph manuscript signed by Rojas on December 9, 1634, *Peligrar en los remedios* was performed on April 6 of the following year in the Royal Palace. It was later published in Rojas' *Primera parte* of 1640. As yet we do not know enough about the chronology of Rojas' plays to speak with certainty, but from the evidence available, *Peligrar* would seem to be one of his earliest individual plays. Only *Persiles y Segismunda* and *El primer Marqués de Astorga* are known to have been composed earlier, although it is likely that *No hay ser padre siendo rey* (performed on January 1, 1635) preceded it, and there were probably several other earlier ones whose titles or dates have eluded us. At any rate, the relatively early date of *Peligrar* is significant because the play marks a definite stage in Rojas' development as a dramatist.

Peligrar en los remedios possesses many of the characteristics of Rojas' dramaturgy: his handling of plot, his favorite dramatic situations, his exuberant poetry, his characterization (especially of strong-willed, passionate women), his saucy servants, and his avoidance of the sacrifice of an innocent wife on the altar of honor, a wife whom circumstantial evidence makes appear guilty of complicity in an extramarital affair. The tone and mood of much of *Peligrar* are typical of those of an honor tragedy; but the avoidance of honor slayings qualifies it as the first of Rojas' plays of implicit protest against the honor code. In short, one has the feeling that with this play Rojas, for better or worse, established most of the patterns that were to guide his future work.

Four men are in love with Duchess Violante: the king of Naples, his favorite the Marquis Alberto, his brother the Infante Carlos, and the latter's best friend, Count Federico. Violante returns Carlos' love, but none of the four men knows of the others' affection for her. For reasons of state, the king becomes engaged to a Sicilian princess and arranges for Carlos to marry her sister, the Infanta Isabela. He also promises the hand of Violante to the Sicilian ambassador, the Almirante. To avoid these undesirable marriages, Carlos and Violante are secretly wed, for, as they both affirm, heaven endowed them with free will to make their own choices, even if it means disobeying the king.

Because of his attachment to Violante, the king repeatedly postpones the state weddings, in spite of the strong protests of the Almirante and the Infanta. Meanwhile, the Marquis Alberto and Count Federico each bribes Violante's servants to admit them into her home where they are surprised by Carlos. Each claims to have been passing by and to have entered the house in pursuit of a muffled intruder. Because of the darkness, Violante cannot identify the man who tried to molest her nor the one who came to her defense. (This is one of Rojas' favorite situations, occurring also in *La traición busca el castigo, Cada cual lo que le toca,* and, with modifications, in *Sin honra no hay amistad* and *No hay amigo para amigo.*) At first Carlos seems to be convinced of Violante's innocence in the affair, but later when, with menacing severity, he draws his dagger, she thinks that he is going to kill her, and declares that she will confess her guilt. Believing this to be an admission of wrongdoing, he threatens to kill her but checks himself:

> *Pero no te he de matar*
> *Por una palabra, no,*
> *Que tal vez el labio erró*
> *Y yo no me quiero errar.*
> (*BAE,* III, 362a)
> (But I'll not kill you
> Because of one word, no,
> For perhaps your lips erred
> And I do not want to err.)

Violante then explains that her guilt consisted in not confiding to Carlos before their marriage that the king, the marquis, and the count were in love with her and persistently solicited her favors. This admission infuriates Carlos, but Violante, using the same words that Leonor will later use in confronting her irate husband in *La traición busca el castigo,* asks: "What fault is it of mine that I am beautiful?" Carlos, who is no Calderonian husband, then admits that his anger is unwarranted, and criticizes those who are prone to assume that their honor has been outraged before any guilt has been established.

The remainder of Act III (to which Cotarelo objected as improbable and artless)[3] draws to a rapid conclusion. After Carlos schemes to get the marquis and the count into a duel with each other, both men, unaware that their conversation is being overheard by Carlos and the king, allege that they would never have tried to force their attentions on Violante if they had known that she was the Infante's wife. The king comes forth, praises the two men for their "loyalty" to his brother (apparently their designs on Violante matter little), and makes amends to the jilted Sicilian Infanta by offering her his hand.

In summary, *Peligrar en los remedios* is essentially an honor drama because conjugal honor is involved, although not a single death occurs. None of the characters inveighs against the provisions of the honor code (as the husbands in Calderón's honor plays tend to do, although they invariably inflict the *castigo* prescribed by the code), but Rojas' play contains an implicit condemnation of those who, acting on flimsy evidence, put honor before love and compassion.

II *Cada cual lo que le toca*

To this play, probably more than any other, Rojas owes his reputation for his daring and originality in treating conjugal honor. Like *Progne y Filomena,* it differs from the conventional honor dramas in having a woman put to death the offender of her honor, but Rojas' originality does not end here. In *Cada cual,* Isabel is forced by her father to marry Don Luis, although prior to their wedding she warns him that their marriage will bring him unhappiness. Isabel is not the first of Rojas' heroines to protest when their freedom of choice in marriage is violated, nor is she the only one to warn an unwelcome suitor of the disaster that could result from a forced marriage. In *Primero es la honra que el gusto,* also of uncertain date, Leonor is bold enough to tell the persistent Don Juan that such a marriage "will cause your honor a grave misfortune." [4] What is new in the present play is the cause of Isabel's unwillingness to marry Don Luis: she was seduced and abandoned by Don Fernando, who refused to keep his promise to marry her.

Coming into possession of this information shortly after their marriage, Don Luis vacillates over what course he should pursue: should he kill his wife or permit her to go unpunished? He remains irresolute. Don Fernando, who turns out to be his best friend, comes to visit him after a long absence. Ironically, Luis tells him of his plight, asking his help in learning the identity of his wife's former lover. Fernando pledges his aid, but later, after overcoming his scruples, confides to his servant that he is determined to enjoy Isabel's favors again. Isabel rejects his advances, but when Fernando persists, she kills him with her husband's dagger (just as Filomena helps kill her offender with her husband's dagger). In a metaphorical sense Isabel becomes, then, the "physician" of her husband's and her own honor by removing the cause of their "infection." Her final gesture as a dutiful wife in asking the pusillanimous Luis to kill her, if he will, is an empty one indeed.

This is one of several of Rojas' plays with an elaborate comic subplot that parodies the main plot. Here the comic subplot is a mock-tragedy involving Galindo, servant of Don Fernando, and Beltrán and Angela, husband and wife, who are the servants of Don Luis and Isabel. Ironically, immediately after reproaching his master for his treacherous intention to possess Isabel, Galindo himself makes love to Angela, wife of his "best" friend. During the seduction of his wife, Beltrán pretends to be asleep, but although he is witness to his shame, he, like his master, is powerless to act. In anguished asides he describes their love-making but he can do nothing except repeat, "Yo con mi daga en la mano" ("And I, with my dagger in my hand").

Although the *gracioso's* repudiation of the demands of the honor code is rather frequent in Spanish drama, I do not know of any other Spanish play in which the comic subplot is used more effectively to invest the tragic action with irony. Rojas' contemporaries, we are told, expressed their displeasure with *Cada cual* because the heroine was seduced prior to her marriage.[5] One can only conjecture on what they thought of the parody of the tragedy of conjugal honor.

III *La traición busca el castigo*

This play was probably composed in 1637 since there is a reference in it to the royal festivities held in Madrid in February of that year in celebration of the election of Ferdinand III, Philip IV's brother-in-law, as the future emperor of the Holy Roman Empire. It was later translated into French by Alain-René Lesage with the title *Le traître puni* (*The Traitor Punished*), and included in his collection, *Le Théâtre espagnol, ou les meilleures comédies des plus fameux auteurs espagnols* (1700). Lesage's translation was in turn put into English by Sir John Vanbrugh, with the title *The False Friend* (1702).

La traición busca el castigo owes much of its interest to its skillfully constructed plot and to its principal character, Don Andrés de Alvarado, an engaging scoundrel who resembles Tirso de Molina's Don Juan Tenorio on several counts. In the initial scene, Mogicón reproaches his master for making love to every woman he meets, young and old alike. Like Don Juan Tenorio, Don Andrés delights in using deceit to seduce women, rejoicing especially in creating discord between lovers.

An indication of the future conflict occurs when Don García,

Leonor's sweetheart, and Don Félix, her father, come separately
to warn Andrés to stop seeing her. He, of course, has no intention of doing so. Their departure is followed by the arrival of
Don Juan Osorio, just returned from the wars in Flanders where
he and Andrés had been close friends. Don Juan reveals that he
is engaged to marry a Valencian beauty whose portrait captivated
him. Unable to convince his friend of the folly of marriage,
Andrés promises his aid, although he does not learn the name
of the girl, nor does he disclose the name of the woman to whom
he is now attracted. He does admit, however, that he is infatuated with her only because he has been warned to stop
seeing her. Leonor, of course, is the girl in both cases, a fact
Andrés learns when he accompanies Juan to her home. Juan
suspects that Leonor is in love with García, her neighbor, but
the latter has been rejected by her father.

Forced to marry Don Juan against her will, Leonor recounts
to her maid (in the first scene of Act II) the torture of her
wedding night. In its intimacy of detail, it even exceeds the
account which the Condestable gives of his first night with
Blanca in *Casarse por vengarse*. There is nothing else quite like
it in the Spanish theater. García comes to bid Leonor goodbye,
and the last part of their conversation is overheard by Juan.
The latter, who has been summoned home because of his father's
illness, asks Andrés to watch over his wife during his absence.
Now truly infatuated with Leonor since she is forbidden fruit,
Andrés enters her room in the darkness, determined to possess
her. Momentarily, he suffers pangs of conscience, but reasoning
that his intention is as culpable as the crime itself, he finally
resolves to carry out his plan. Leonor's cries attract García, who
rushes in to confront Andrés, but the latter also claims to have
come in answer to her outcry. When Don Juan, who received
news of his father's death as he was about to leave Valencia,
returns unexpectedly, Leonor is unable to identify her aggressor.

Although Juan has cause to suspect Leonor's complicity in
the affair, especially after learning that both García and Andrés
had previously courted her, he takes no action against her but,
contrary to the usual run of honor-conscious husbands, asks her
help in clarifying the case. Finally convinced that García is
the culprit, Don Juan asks Andrés how he should avenge him-

self. Andrés advises him to use the same means that García used to dishonor him: to scale the wall that divides their houses and to kill him furtively in his home. In the darkness, however, Don Juan mistakenly kills his false friend, who confesses his guilt before dying.

A possible source of *La traición busca el castigo* is Guillén de Castro's *Donde no está su dueño está su duelo*, although the situations which the two plays have in common are not unusual in the period. In both plays the husband is obliged to absent himself from his bride. Accordingly, he encourages his best friend, who is secretly infatuated with his wife, to look after her during his absence. The false friend attempts to possess the woman by force, whereupon the husband returns unexpectedly to find circumstantial evidence indicating that his wife had adulterous intentions. The husband does not act hastily, however, but gives his wife the opportunity to exonerate herself, which she does successfully. Here the resemblance ends. In Castro's plays the friend admits his evil intentions and is pardoned by the husband, whereas in Rojas' the false friend falls victim to the trap he has laid for an innocent man whom he unjustly accuses of the offense.

Although *La traición busca el castigo* is usually classified as a tragedy of conjugal honor, that classification is inaccurate because the husband takes no action against his wife although he has reason to suspect her, nor is the offender killed intentionally. Perhaps it would be more accurate to call it a tragedy of retribution because it bears out that biblical admonition, "Whosoever maketh a pit for others shall fall into it himself: for his mischief will return upon his own head, and his cruelty fall upon his own pate." (Psalms vii, 16–17)

IV *Casarse por vengarse*

All but forgotten today, *Casarse por vengarse* was one of Rojas' most influential plays outside of Spain in the seventeenth and eighteenth centuries. Not only was it imitated in dramatic form but it also served as the source of Alain-René Lesage's *novella*, "Le Mariage de vengeance," included in his renowned novel, *Gil Blas* (1715–1735). Lesage's *novella* became in turn the source of several dramatic compositions, including Carlo Goldoni's *Enrico re di Sicilia* (1737).[6]

One of the few modern critics to mention Rojas' play is Valbuena Prat, who speaks of it as "a violent drama with a rather forced, uneven style, although possessing great beauty in some of its parts." [7] The Spanish critic goes on to say that its unmistakable model was Calderón's *El médico de su honra* which was first performed in 1635, a year before Rojas' drama was first printed. In spite of a few general similarities between the two plays, however, *Casarse por vengarse* reveals its own originality and emotional intensity. It stands as one of the best examples of Rojas' great talent for writing persuasively of the bliss and sorrows of love.

Reared in the home of Don Roberto, Enrique, prince of Sicily, and Blanca, Roberto's daughter, have long been sweethearts. They are "two entwined flowers" that cannot live apart. When King Rugero dies, his will stipulates that Enrique is to succeed to the throne only on the condition that he marry his cousin Rosaura. Enrique pretends to accept Rosaura, but promises Blanca that he will never marry anyone but her. Desiring to abide by the deceased king's wishes, Don Roberto offers Blanca's hand to the Condestable who has asked to marry her. Blanca, feeling that Enrique has betrayed her, agrees to the marriage "to take revenge on herself," as she puts it, for having loved him.

After her marriage Enrique continues to visit Blanca by means of a secret partition in her room, although she attempts to discourage him. With an intimacy rare in the Golden Age theater, the Condestable confides to Don Roberto that when Blanca and he retired to their nuptial bed after the wedding, instead of being receptive to his caresses she broke into sobs, and that later he brushed against a man in the darkness of her room. Don Roberto assures him that Blanca's apparent coolness was caused by maidenly modesty, but applauds him for being alert to the defense of his honor. However, the Condestable becomes convinced of his wife's guilt when he later overhears her talking to Enrique.

After discovering the secret partition, the Condestable determines to make use of it to avenge his honor, as it was used to dishonor him. Learning that Enrique is coming to see Blanca that night, he has her write a letter while sitting at a desk opposite the partition. When Enrique approaches, the Condestable crashes the partition upon her head, killing her. Enrique enters to find the husband lamenting the tragic accident which he says he cannot explain. This type of ironic dénouement in which the instrument of an offense becomes the instrument of the offender's punishment was cultivated by Rojas and by his European contemporaries who wrote tragedies of revenge. It involves the same kind of retribution or "justice" approved by Othello when Iago opposes his plan to poison Desdemona:

IAGO:
Do it not with poison; strangle her in her bed, even the bed she hath contaminated.

OTHELLO:
Good, good; the justice of it pleases, very good.

(*Othello,* IV, vv. 220 ff.)

Although *Casarse por vengarse* utilizes many devices of cape-and-sword drama (the secret partition, fortuitous encounters and escapes, eavesdropping, intercepted letters, etc.), it deserves attention because of its rapturous love poetry, its frank portrayal of marital intimacies, and its bold characterization, especially of Blanca, who, as the title suggests, would rather be dead than wed.

V *Del rey abajo, ninguno*

It is ironical that Rojas, who is noted for his unusual treatment of the honor theme, is remembered chiefly for an honor drama, *Del rey abajo, ninguno*, long recognized as one of the masterpieces of the Spanish theater. As already mentioned, there is some doubt concerning the authorship of this play which was first printed under the name of Calderón in *Parte cuarenta y dos de comedias de diferentes autores* (Zaragoza, 1651).[8] No record of its performance in the seventeenth century has been preserved, but it was often reprinted in the eighteenth and enjoyed a revival on the stage during the first four decades of the nineteenth century. One enthusiastic critic writing in the latter period despaired of classifying it by genre because, he said, it could be neither tragedy, comedy, drama, nor melodrama (perhaps a good argument for claiming that the Spanish *comedia* is *sui generis*). He then echoed the Englishman who, incensed because critics refused to concede that Milton's *Paradise Lost* is an epic poem, called it a "divine work." [9]

As the play begins, Don Mendo urges King Alfonso XI to grant his petition to make him a knight in the military order of the *Banda*. The king is making preparations for his campaign against the Moors in Algeciras. Surprised by the generosity of a supposed peasant, García de Castañar, who has written him pledging money and provisions, the king questions the Count of Orgaz about him. His curiosity aroused by the count's praise, Alfonso decides to go incognito to see his loyal vassal. He is accompanied by Don Mendo, who wears the red band of the Order to which he has just been appointed.

In Castañar, where he conceals his noble blood because of a political misunderstanding between his father and the former king, García leads the life of a rich peasant, dividing his time between overseeing his lands and hunting. Deeply in love with his wife Blanca, García has no desire to return to the court. He envies no man. Informed by the Count of Orgaz that a royal party will soon visit him and that the king "es el de la banda roja," García welcomes his guests, inviting them to dine. Because of the red band worn by Don Mendo, he takes him to be the king. Don Mendo becomes infatuated with Blanca, but when she remains cool to his attentions, he resolves to return to Castañar when her husband is absent. One night when García is hunting, the courtier enters Blanca's room by means of a ladder. García returns to find Mendo in the room, but still believing him to be the king, permits him to leave.

Convinced that the king has tried to dishonor him, García is torn between loyalty to his monarch and the demands of the honor code. Unable to take revenge on the king, whose person was inviolable, García sees no alternative but to kill Blanca, although he has no doubt of her innocence.

Overcome by grief when he attempts to kill her, García loses consciousness momentarily. She escapes and meets the Count of

Orgaz, who sends her to the court in Toledo. There, informed of her noble lineage, the queen entrusts her to the protection of Don Mendo, who continues to importune her. García arrives to take her away but is prevented from doing so by Don Mendo. When King Alfonso appears, García realizes that he has mistaken the identity of the two men. He then leaves with his offender and kills him in an adjoining room. Upon hearing the circumstances of the case and the reasons García assumed the guise of a peasant, the king pardons him. García speaks the final lines, swearing to bathe the Moors of Algeciras in blood.

Several earlier plays have been cited as possible sources of the drama, among them Lope de Vega's *Peribáñez y el comendador de Ocaña* and *El villano en su rincón*, Luis Vélez de Guevara's *La luna de la sierra*, and Tirso de Molina's *El celoso prudente*.[10] It is Lope's two plays, however, that influenced Rojas most. Written about 1610, *Peribáñez* has as hero and heroine a peasant couple, Peribáñez and Casilda, who, like García and Blanca, are devoted to each other. Their idyllic existence is threatened when the Comendador becomes enamoured of Casilda and invents a ruse to send her husband away so that he can make love to her. On discovering that the Comendador has tried to force himself on his wife, Peribáñez loses no time in killing his offender. Informed of the events in the case, the king pardons the peasant on the grounds that he was defending his honor.

Joseph Fucilla, among others, has also pointed out the similarity between *Del rey abajo, ninguno* and Lope's *El villano en su rincón*, especially with regard to the characterization of the two protagonists and their intense loyalty to the king.[11] Juan Labrador in Lope's play, like García, has never seen the king but holds him in veneration; also like García he contributes liberally to his sovereign's needs. In both plays the king, surprised by the generosity of his lowly subjects, goes incognito to visit them. Both Juan Labrador and García del Castañar speak eloquently before their royal guest of the superiority of country life over life at court—and here the resemblance between the plays ends.

Indeed, one of the major themes of Rojas' play is the *beatus ille*, the "blessed is the man" theme cultivated by Horace and Virgil in antiquity and favored by pastoral poets and novelists in the Renaissance who charged their readers to return to nature's untrammeled precincts. Perhaps the most ardent statement of the contrast between court and country is found in Antonio de Guevara's *Del menosprecio de la corte y alabanza de la aldea* (1539), whose English translation by Sir Francis Bryan, *A Dispraise of the Life of a Courtier and a Commendation of the Life of a Labouryng Man* (1548), underscores the corrupting influence of court life and the wholesome environment of the farmer. Of course, in Rojas' play this contrast is represented by Don Mendo, the frivolous, self-seeking courtier, and García, the magnanimous man of the soil.

One of the chief problems in the composition of *Del rey abajo, ninguno* was to create poetry capable of sustaining its theme of the transcendent beauty of country life. How well the dramatist succeeded is set forth in an important article on the poetry of the play by Bruce Wardropper, who writes: "One might define this poetic world, roughly, as one in which all living things vie with one another, each striving to outdo the other in beauty and perfection. But since the rivalry is an equal struggle each advantage is not gained at the expense of another creature: if the beech and the oak compete to gain greater height, the whole forest is that much nearer its goal of reaching the sky; if a girl's beauty exceeds the previously established acme of beauty, the ideal of beauty is enhanced. This, then, is a world of progressively increasing beauty and perfection, but one that remains always in harmony. It is the Platonic pastoral transfigured and magnified without detriment to the Platonic ideal of harmony." [12]

The contrast between court and country, between courtier and peasant, is related to another important theme: the difference between appearance and reality.[13] This theme begins in the initial scene when Don Mendo asks the king to make him a knight of the *Banda*. Apparently, the courtier is a man of exceptional merit, since investigation has proved that he is of good blood and he has served faithfully in the royal palace for ten years. Accordingly, the king awards him the coveted red band which not only leads to García's confusion concerning the identity of the king but also becomes the external—and deceitful —sign of Don Mendo's nobility. Later events prove that he lacks the inner virtues appropriate to the insignia he wears.

At the same time that the ambitious Mendo is asking for favors, the generous García, by means of his letter, offers to help the king to the extent of his capabilities. For this reason, the king decides to go to Castañar to discover a "hidden treasure." In effect, throughout the play Don Mendo shows off his nobility of lineage and acts ignobly, while García, the supposed peasant, conceals his nobility and acts nobly. The interplay of appearance and reality continues until the final scene when García, after killing Mendo, reveals why he has lived disguised as a peasant, an account which the Count of Orgaz verifies as, "Truths which must be revealed." [14] Again, the poetry of the play, with its insistence upon images of external appearance and hidden value, enriches the theme.

But what makes *Del rey abajo, ninguno* an especially moving drama is the manner in which the author dramatizes the conflict between two Spanish ideals, loyalty to the king and personal honor. In his *Historia del teatro español*, Valbuena Prat devotes a chapter (XIV) to what he calls "El conflicto con los poderes de la tierra," [15] a conflict between an individual's loyalty to the king and his personal values. Earlier dramatists often exploited the drama and pathos inherent in this conflict, but rarely in a play of conjugal honor is the conflict dramatized so poignantly as here. The key to the intensity of the conflict lies in the care with which the author develops García's loyalty to the king, and, at the same time, the love of García and Blanca. The duo of sonnets exchanged between them (beginning in verse 291), despite the conventionality of their form and occurrence, captures the depth of their mutual devotion. It is no wonder, then, that when García is faced with the terrible necessity of killing his wife he cannot steel himself to commit the act and "blacks out."

Although the basic conflict in *Del rey abajo, ninguno* may lack reality for modern readers who cannot comprehend how a vassal's loyalty to the king can force him to consider the murder of an adored wife, those who project themselves into the spirit of the times cannot fail to be moved by the intensity of that conflict.

CHAPTER 5

The Religious Plays
and Autos Sacramentales

I The Religious Plays

R OJAS was not, as far as one can tell from what is known about his life or from his plays, a deeply religious man. Although his sins were probably not as many or great as Lope de Vega's, neither was he seized by religious fervor or moved to spiritual ecstasy as Lope often was.[1] Nor did he have the theocentric sense of life that emerges so vividly from many of Calderón's plays. Rojas was, in short, a rather secular-minded man, and the wonder of it is that he bothered to write religious plays at all.

To be sure, many seventeenth-century plays of religious subject matter fail to communicate a religious sense or meaning. Whether they are edifying or not depends entirely upon the author's treatment of his material. Saints' plays, it has been observed, often follow a common formula: after leading a scandalous life, the protagonist, endowed with God's grace and touched by His mercy, experiences a sudden conversion. If he is martyred, so much the better (for the play at least) because his death comes as a spectacular *coup de théâtre*. The saint's miracles and apotheosis are usually attended by supernatural doings often involving the elaborate use of stage machinery. But if a saint's play does no more than provide "good theater," if it does not create a vision of the truth that illuminates the protagonist, it is poor religious propaganda. One has the impression that Rojas was too often concerned with creating effect rather than revealing a perception of truth.

Los trabajos de Tobías

Rojas' only biblical play is drawn from the Book of Tobías,

although he also knew Lope de Vega's *La historia de Tobías,* printed in 1621. Since Rojas retains most of the events and characters of the biblical story, a summary of it is in order. Tobias, a paragon of piety, charity, and patience, is continuously in difficulty with friend and foe because of his insistence upon burying the dead. While dispensing charity to other unfortunates, he is blinded by a swallow's droppings, but he cheerfully accepts his blindness as a manifestation of God's will. After giving his son (also named Tobias) good moral counsel, he sends him from Ninive to Rages to collect a debt from Gabelus.

Accompanied by the disguised angel Raphael, the younger Tobias catches a fish in the Tigris whose liver and gall he keeps on the advice of his companion. In Rages he meets and falls in love with Sara, daughter of Raguel, his father's kinsman. Raguel is reluctant to agree to the young couple's marriage because his daughter is the victim of a strange curse: she has been married seven times and on each occasion her new husband has dropped dead on the wedding night. (Rojas has her neighbors call her *matamaridos* ["husband killer"].) But Tobias in Ninive and Sara in Rages bear their afflictions with resignation, praying that God's will be done.

Having secured Raguel's permission for their marriage, the young Tobias and Sara spend their first three nights together in constant prayer. Sara's relatives, who have already dug a grave for the bridegroom, are surprised to find him still alive; but he has succeeded in warding off the devil Asmodeo, who killed Sara's previous husbands who approached her in lust, by burning the fish's liver. After a wedding feast, the young Tobias and Sara return to Ninive, where on Raphael's advice, the son anoints his father's eyes with the fish's gall, restoring his sight. After revealing his identity, the angel Raphael informs father and son that they have found favor with God because of their piety and faith. Tobias the elder lives to a ripe hundred and two years of age; Tobias the younger lives to be ninety-nine, "and he saw his children's children to the fifth generation."

In his dramatization of the biblical story, Rojas probably did his utmost to capture the piety of the principal characters, but the few critics who have commented on the play have not been able to agree on the results. Menéndez y Pelayo terms it "a monstruous play, altisonant and gongoristic, without a trace of poetry or mystic sentiment"; [2] while Cotarelo finds it filled with "poetic tenderness." [3] Cotarelo goes on to say that the continual infractions of the unity of place were what obliged the author to use two stages in part of the play.[4] Neither critic seems to have been sympathetic with the fact that *Los trabajos de Tobías* involves a bold experiment with dramatic structure and staging.

The biblical story contains two actions, widely separated in space, which are unified thematically by the sufferings and piety of the principal character in each. One action involves Tobias' life in Ninive—and a hard life it is, the way Rojas dramatizes it. In Act II, after having wandered naked and hungry for a month, Tobias is given shelter by a kind Assyrian who also gives refuge to other homeless souls. Given a piece of bread by his benefactor, the starving Tobias starts to eat it when a dog snatches it and runs away. Refusing to retrieve the bread from one of God's creatures, Tobias is rebuked by his host for his seeming ingratitude. Other indignities are heaped upon the hapless man. A *mujer pobre* sings a song mocking his suffering. A swallow defecates in his eyes, blinding him. Morrión, the *gracioso* who pretends to be blind in one eye, taunts him. Another *pobre* demands his shoes which Tobias cheerfully surrenders. Finally, he escapes by going on an act of mercy: guided by his wife he goes to bury a corpse which the others refuse to touch. All these incidents are crowded into a single scene, a grotesque scene of jolting contrasts between Tobias' charity and patience and his tormentors' cruelty.

The second action involves Sara's life in Rages. A devout maiden, she would like to preserve her virginity, but her father forces her to marry Joseph (whom Rojas creates as a rival to the younger Tobias for her love). Although Joseph is warned to remain continent for three days following the wedding, he cannot restrain his passion. He orders the tearful bride to prepare herself for him, whereupon Asmodeo comes to kill the lustful husband. Sara's afflictions are certainly of a different order from those of Tobias, but she bears them with the same resignation to God's will.

In order to achieve parallelism and an effect of simultaneousness between the two actions, Rojas employs the common technique of alternating scenes between them—but he also goes much farther. He uses two stages so that the spectators can see the events occurring simultaneously in each action. At the end of Act II, Tobias on one stage in Ninive and Sara on the other in Rages engage in a kind of antiphonal dialogue, recounting their ordeals and praying in alternating sequence. At the same time two angels (who also comment in antiphonal dialogue on their piety) record their words to carry them to God.[5] Rojas' use of two stages was not motivated, as Cotarelo thought, by the need to resolve difficulties arising from the violation of the classical unity of place (which Spanish dramatists disregarded at every turn anyway). Rather, their use represents a deliberate effort to achieve a unity greater than that of space by bringing into simultaneous view distant characters who are unified in their devotion to God.

Menéndez y Pelayo may have been right in saying that *Los trabajos de Tobías* lacks mystic sentiment, but in none of his other religious plays did Rojas try so hard to capture the pain and exaltation of God-fearing souls.

El mejor amigo el muerto (El capuchino escocés)

This play should not be confused with *El mejor amigo el muerto,* written in collaboration by Luis de Belmonte, Rojas, and Calderón, which has the subtitle *Fortunas de don Juan de Castro* and which is a recast of Lope de Vega's two-part play, *Don Juan de Castro.*[6] The subtitle of Rojas' individual play occurs in altered form in the closing lines: "So ends here The Dead Man as the Best Friend and the Scotch Capuchin" ("Conque fin aquí ha tenido/ El mejor amigo el muerto/ y el escocés capuchino . . ."). According to Cotarelo, the source of the play is *La historia de Fray Arcángel de Escocia,* contained in the histories of the Capuchin order written by Salucio and Carlos de Aremberg.[7] The play is preserved only in an undated manuscript in the Biblioteca Nacional (No. 15671). There is no record of its having been performed, but I suspect that it was composed during that period in the 1640's when secular plays were banned from Spanish theaters.

The play deals with the conversion of Jorge Lesleo, a young

Scot who is to go to Paris to continue his studies of Calvinistic doctrine. Prior to his departure he falls asleep while reading a book on Calvinism, whereupon his friend Enrique, a Catholic, enters and discloses that he will seek his friend's salvation. He substitutes for the book Jorge has in his hand another on the life of Saint Francis, about which Jorge exclaims in his sleep, "This is the one of truth." Furious when he learns that Enrique intends to convert his son to Catholicism, Jacobo Lesleo kills him, leaving Jorge to bemoan the loss of his "mejor amigo el muerto."

In Paris, Enrique's ghost appears to Jorge, exhorting him to abandon his heresy, but Jorge, offended, rejects him. Enamored of Blanca, who he does not know is the sister of his friend Carlos, Jorge goes to her room to keep an appointment with her. When he is on the verge of entering the room, Enrique's ghost appears again, prepared to prove that he is his best friend. The ghost unlocks the door, whereupon Carlos suddenly appears and "kills" him. Convinced by this evidence of Enrique's friendship, Jorge resolves to abandon his false religion and follow that of his dead friend.

After taking orders and adopting the name Arcángelo, Jorge returns to Scotland where he visits his father who grieves over his son's defection; however, he helps him escape when voices are heard calling for the blood of the papist. In the nearby woods, Jorge relates to his father and Aurora, his former sweetheart, the story of his conversion. Moved by this account, both renounce their heresy. Saint Francis, accompanied by Enrique, appears to accept the converts into the fold and to assign new duties to Fray Arcángelo.

In an effort to enliven this dull play, Rojas employs two comical devices, the first a common one in the *comedias de santos,* the other a farcical interlude characteristic of the dramatist. Pierres, Carlos' French servant, takes holy orders at the same time as Jorge and becomes his constant companion. However, like Lagartija in Cervantes' *El rufián dichoso* (and like many other servants who follow their masters in choosing a religious vocation), he is reluctant to renounce his fondness for food and drink, and constantly grumbles about his sacrifices. But this common comic device was not enough for Rojas. As in several other plays, he created an enema-minded enemy for Pierres, a Scotch *vejete* who spends most of his time on the stage chasing Pierres with a syringe. The frightened Frenchman gains revenge on the Scot by duping him into believing he is blind and collecting a large sum of money to restore his sight. These comical intrusions do little to enliven *El mejor amigo el muerto,* and perhaps it is just as well that Rojas probably never wrote the second part promised in the closing lines of the play.

Nuestra Señora de Atocha y segundo Jepté

Preserved in an autograph manuscript (Res. 61 in the Biblioteca Nacional), this play was finished and signed by Rojas on February 11, 1639. It was later published in the *Segunda parte* of his plays printed in 1645. The precise source of the play is not known, but the legend of the Patroness of Madrid was contained in various chronicles and religious literature. Numerous writers, before and after Rojas, treated the same legend in poetry and plays.[8] One of the best known poetic treatments composed during Rojas' lifetime was Alfonso Jerónimo de Salas Barbadillo's *Patrona de Madrid restituyda* (Madrid, 1609), a poem consisting of 733 octaves. As previously mentioned (in Chapter 1), Rojas' reason for dramatizing the legend was an all-compelling one: Philip IV, whom the playwright was always anxious to please, was especially devoted to Nuestra Señora de Atocha. It is not unlikely that Rojas' play was written for a special celebration in her honor.

According to legend, the image of Our Lady of Atocha was brought to Madrid from Antioch in the early days of Christianity by the disciples of Saint Peter or by the Prince of the Apostles himself. In the year 719 or thereabouts, Madrid was surrendered to the Moors, with the understanding that the hermitage which housed the image was to be respected. Gracián Ramírez, mayor of Madrid and an ardent devotee of Our Lady, was distressed to learn that the image had disappeared. After a long search, it was found in a field of bassweed (*atochar*) near the Manzanares River. Rather than return the image to its former site, Gracián Ramírez decided to build a new sanctuary where it was found, but the Moors, thinking that the Christians were erecting new fortifications, assembled an army to attack them. As the Moorish army approached, Gracián Ramírez, fearful of the fate that awaited his wife and two daughters, decided to kill them to spare them from dishonor, a decision with which they concurred. Accordingly, he beheaded them and left their bodies at the foot of the altar of Our Lady.[9]

Soon after, the Virgin of Atocha appeared to lead the Christians to victory over the Moors. As the Christians made their way to the sanctuary to give thanks for their deliverance, Gracián Ramírez berated himself for not having sufficient faith to believe that she would have protected his family. Upon entering the sanctuary, he was overcome with joy to see his wife and daughters kneeling in prayer before the altar, the sword marks still visible on their throats. The Christians then paraded the image of the Virgin of Atocha in triumph through the streets of the reconquered town, proclaiming her the Patroness of Madrid.

Around this pious legend Rojas fabricated a series of romantic adventures involving Gracián Ramírez' daughters, Leonor and Elvira, who not so piously bicker over the love of García and Fernando. Both men, unfortunately, prefer Leonor. To top it off, Fernando is captured by the Moors and becomes the reluctant object of the affections of Rosa, sister of the Moorish king of Toledo. In a reversal to an incident of plot in *El Abencerraje,* Rosa releases Fernando in order that he may visit his sweetheart. In addition to leaving a portrait of Leonor as a pledge, he swears by the Holy Gospels, the Cross, and Saint James that he will return to captivity. However, reunited with Leonor in Madrid, he allows himself to be persuaded to forget his promise, since she argues that he now possesses the real Leonor and not just her likeness. Although Fernando does not redeem his pledge (a fact which disturbs his sense of honor a bit), he is given an opportunity to repay Rosa for her kindness when, later in the play, she and her brother are on the verge of being killed by vengeful Christians. He gallantly covers their retreat, allowing them to escape. At the end of the play Fernando gets Leonor, and García is matched with Elvira.

A peculiar feature of *Nuestra Señora de Atocha* is that much of it, like Lope de Vega's *Las famosas asturianas,* is written in old Spanish. Only the Moors speak modern Castilian. This device, designed to capture the spirit of the epoch, does lend quaintness to the play, but does not compensate for the many ruses with which Rojas complicates the plot. Despite these ruses, however, Cotarelo admired the play because he thought it captured well the devotion and heroism of the early Castilians.[10]

Santa Isabel, reina de Portugal

Saint Isabel (1271–1336), princess of Aragon and queen of Portugal, was approved for canonization by Pope Urban VIII in May of 1625, thanks largely to the efforts of Philip IV. It is not surprising, therefore, that Rojas, who was ever alert to the devotions (and caprices) of his sovereign, should write a play concerning her. The play was performed at the Royal Palace, probably on September 18, 1635, although as mentioned earlier there is some doubt about the date.[11]

Critics could find nothing good to say about the play until Edward Glaser made a penetrating study of it a few years ago.[12] Glaser also pointed out its principal source: Fray Juan Carrillo, *Historia, y vida de Santa Isabel Reyna de Portugal, y infanta de Aragón* (Zaragoça, 1617). It also contains, I would suggest, incidents drawn from two plays of Rojas' friend and collaborator, Luis Vélez de Guevara: *El privado perseguido,* known also as *El lucero de Castilla y luna de Aragón,* and *De la devoción de la misa.* As was his custom, however, Rojas exercised a free hand with both his historical and literary sources.

Forced by her father to become the wife of King Dionís of Portugal although she much preferred to be a Sister of Saint Francis, Isabel has a tough time with her husband. He philanders, he nags her for her unqueenly dress, he opposes her works of charity, and, what is worse, goaded by the insinuations of his villainous favorite, Carlos (a kind of English Iago in Portugal's service), he suspects her of having illicit relations with her secretary, Ramiro. Nor do Ramiro and Carlos get along well. Not only are they divided by political and personal loyalties but they are also rivals for the love of Blanca. Their enmity constitutes a subplot which parallels the constant misunderstandings of the king and queen in the main plot.

In order to effect a reconciliation after one of their quarrels, the king gives his wife a necklace which she in turn gives to Ramiro to help the poor. His suspicions "confirmed" when he sees Ramiro wearing the necklace (a variation of the motif of Desdemona's handkerchief), the king resolves to kill his offenders. He orders Ramiro to deliver a letter personally to the addressee, but the secretary is prevented from doing so when he is diverted by a pious mission. Carlos schemes to deliver it, thinking that it will bring him a reward. Later, intent on murdering his wife, the king enters her room but his hand is stayed when he finds her, dressed in religious habit, praying before a crucifix. At this point, a worker arrives to report to the king that he carried out the instructions of the letter: he threw the bearer into a kiln of quick-lime after hearing his confession that he had been disloyal to the king.[13] The latter is amazed when Ramiro returns unharmed, but realizes that poetic justice has been done when he learns how Carlos conspired to procure the letter. The *gracioso* makes the final speech, announcing that Ramiro will marry Blanca and promising a second part of the play which, apparently, was never written.

In his study of the play, Glaser points out that Rojas departs from the previous literature on Saint Isabel in particular and from the usual concern of saints' plays in general. Always interested in feminine psychology, Rojas does not emphasize the supernatural acts associated with the saintly queen but underscores her human qualities as a woman and a wife. The plot does not hinge upon her miracles but on her efforts to resolve a problem of conjugal honor. Nor is much attention given to religious doctrine. Here, as in his other religious plays, Rojas was interested in drama, not dogma.

La vida en el ataúd

The most rewarding of Rojas' religious plays, at least for its drama if not for its piety, *La vida en el ataúd* was first printed in *Parte 32* of *Comedias nuevas, nunca impresas, escogidas de los mejores ingenios de España* (Madrid, 1669). Its date of composition is not known, nor is there any record of its having been performed, although again, it may have been written and staged in the 1640's when secular plays were banned. Its probable source is the account of Saint Boniface's martyrdom contained in Pedro de Ribadeneira's *Flos Sanctorum o Libro de las vidas de los santos* (Barcelona, 1623).[14]

According to Ribadeneira's biography, during the early years of the fourth century Bonifacio served as majordomo in the household of Aglaes, a young Roman noblewoman of resplendent beauty but lamentable morals. Enamored of her servant, Aglaes regaled him with money and her charms, a fact which incensed her relatives and scandalized Roman society. Despite his dissolute personal life, however, Bonifacio had positive virtues: he was gentle and compassionate by nature, and he spent much of his mistress' money to help the poor. Finally, moved by God's mercy, Aglaes and Bonifacio repented for their wicked ways, resolving to earn forgiveness by redeeming the bodies of Christians martyred by the Roman pagans. Accordingly, provided with a large sum of money by Aglaes, Bonifacio went to Tarsus where, after comforting a group of tortured Christians, he was seized, tormented, and beheaded.

Remembering his unsavory past, his friends attributed his absence to dalliance but later they found his corpse and head. They joined the two parts together, and "the saintly martyr opened his eyes and looked at them lovingly with a happy face. . . . as if he pardoned them for what they had thought and said about him." [15] They redeemed the body and set sail for Rome where an angel appeared to Aglaes telling her to receive Bonifacio as a martyr of Christ. The biography concludes with an account of the saint's burial, the miracles performed in behalf of his devotees, and Aglaes' exemplary conduct during her remaining years.

Around this pious history Rojas constructed a plot which includes several non-historical situations: the rivalry of Aglaes and Milene (a character invented by Rojas) for the love of the young nobleman, Arnesto, the refusal of the two girls to marry suitors selected by their families, and, after the death of Arnesto, their rivalry for Bonifacio's love. It is their rivalry, sustained throughout most of the play, which provides the basic conflict of the plot. Bonifacio's conversion and martyrdom occupy only the latter part of the final act.

Most voluptuous of all Rojas' heroines, Aglaes is typical of his passionate, strong-willed women who let nothing stand in the way of their desires. Upon regaining consciousness after a fall from a horse, she embraces Bonifacio, thinking he is her sweetheart Arnesto. Chagrined to discover that the man in her arms is her servant whom she hardly noticed before, Aglaes rebukes him but remains obsessed by the warmth of his touch. Later, when her friend Milene also becomes infatuated with the slave, they vie with one another to gratify the passion he has ignited in them, although both women remonstrate with themselves for loving a man of such humble station. But Milene is no match for Aglaes, who, having overcome all scruples of class ("Viva yo a mi gusto/ y ríase el mundo," [16] she says in a paraphrase of Góngora's well-known *letrilla*), entices Bonifacio to her bedroom where she seduces the future saint.

The third act begins with one of the most sensual scenes in Spanish drama. As dawn comes to disturb the languor of the lovers spent by their night's play, they have this conversation (translated in the Notes):

BONIFACIO:
  No he visto sol más necio . . .

AGLAES:
  Vete, vete; que siento
  pasos en la antecámara.

BONIFACIO:
                              No, apenas
  en ella bulle el viento;
  duerme, señora, un poco.

AGLAES:
                              Pues lo ordenas,
  no pretendo eximirme,
  aunque en tus brazos tengo de dormirme . . .

BONIFACIO:
  Reposad y dormid, ojos serenos.

AGLAES:
  ¿Estás ahí?

BONIFACIO:
            Dejarte
  en blando sueño sepultada quiero.

[90]

AGLAES:
> Duermo por agradarte,
> aunque no duermo; que de amores muero,
> que es dormir de otra suerte,
> glorioso padecer y dulce muerte.

BONIFACIO:
> Duerme, duerme. La vida
> deposito en tus manos.

BONIFACIO:
>   Dulcemente
> se ha quedado dormida.

AGLAES:
> Vete, mi bien . . .   (Entre sueños.)

BONIFACIO:
> Descansad y dormid, ojos serenos.

AGLAES:
> ¿Dónde estoy? [17]

So ends this scene of sexual ecstasy. While still asleep, Aglaes has a vision of her martyred lover (a jolting juxtaposition of baroque sensuality and spirituality), but she is comforted when an angel appears to tell her that she will acquire salvation as a result of Bonifacio's death. Onorato, uncle of Aglaes, threatens to kill Bonifacio for having dishonored him through Aglaes, but when Bonifacio admits his guilt and refuses to defend himself, Onorato permits him to go to Tarsus. The rest of the act concerns Bonifacio's martyrdom, the triumphal return of his body to Rome, and the conversion of Aglaes, Milene, and Candor, the *gracioso*.

La vida en el ataúd offers a striking example of a saint's play in which the religious element, whether or no it was the author's intention, is subordinated to the secular. Although there are isolated scenes throughout the play depicting the Christians' struggle to defend their faith, although sins of the flesh lead to repentance and salvation, although, as so often in saints' plays, God's great mercy lifts a sinner, inexplicably, to holy martyrdom, the enduring delectability of the love scenes all but obscures any pious purposes Rojas may have had in writing the play.

El profeta falso Mahoma

One of Rojas' weakest plays, *El profeta falso Mahoma* may be classified among the religious dramas only because of the fact that it involves a conflict between Moslems and Christians over doctrinal matters. Composed of three virtually unrelated plots and numerous disjointed scenes, it resembles nothing else so much as a patchwork in the writing of which various collaborators failed to put their heads together. There is no question of its authenticity, however, since it was published in the author's *Primera parte* of 1640. Even Cotarelo, who was often so benevolent toward Rojas' lapses, thought the play unworthy of him.[18]

Mahoma (Mohammed), the ready-made villain of this melodrama, comports himself as foully as any Spanish audience could desire. There are few crimes that the wicked prophet has not committed, as he confesses in recounting his rise to power: He has cheated and defrauded, he has sold his soul to the devil in exchange for powers of magic, and he intends to kill his henchman Sergio. Moreover, he secretly acknowledges Christ as the true God. This is Mahoma's dilemma: Should he, with the help of his demon allies, continue to enjoy the plush days until they call for his soul, or should he give the lie to his false claims, seeking salvation through Christ? For a moment toward the end of the play, Mahoma engages in serious introspection as he ponders over his inability to dominate his passions and rectify his errors; but he, of course, remains an unregenerate villain. He tries to win over his Christian adversaries by a display of magic, but when they call upon the Cross, he falls from a cloud and is mortally wounded. The final lines assure us that all is well because the scoundrel has received his due.

The best thing about this play is the *gracioso* Testuz, a Christian masquerading as a Mohammedan. Giving a long account of his lineage as an excuse for violating the prohibition against eating pork and drinking wine, he claims to be a member of the Puerco, Marrano, and Lechón families (Hog, Boar, and Pig families). He also claims that he is "the finest wine taster from the North to the South Pole." Testuz is as good as his word. In a parody of the legend of the Siete Infantes de Lara, he "kills off" seven *botas* of famous Spanish wines. Then, like the bereaved Gonzalo Gustioz lamenting over the heads of his seven sons, he pronounces a tender eulogy over the lifeless forms of each of the *hermanitos*: Esquivias, Valdemoro, Toro, Abaejos, Burguillos, Ajofrín, and Membrilla. No *gracioso* ever put on a more heart-rending drinking scene.

II *The* Autos Sacramentales

Since most of Rojas' religious plays possess little spiritual substance and less doctrinal content, one would not expect him to be a successful writer of *autos sacramentales* because of the peculiar demands made on the dramatist by that genre. His first *auto, El Hércules,* was written for the Corpus Christi celebrations held in Madrid in 1639 when it was presented together with two of Calderón's (*Santa María Egipciaca* and *El mejor huésped de España*) and one of Antonio Coello's (*La cárcel del mundo*).[19] From that time until his death in 1648 he is known to have written nine *autos sacramentales,* although several others have been attributed to him. Since dramatists were relatively well paid for *autos,* it is fair to say that his efforts in the genre were more successful financially than artistically.

Rojas had neither the head nor the heart for writing *autos.* He had a smattering of scholastic philosophy, in which all Spanish university students were schooled, but he lacked knowledge and control of dogmatic theology. He had little feeling for liturgy; he was not at ease working with allegory. Although most of his *autos* involve the eucharistic theme, he was unable to dramatize the significance of the sacrament of Holy Communion. In short, Rojas' *autos* are deficient in content and form.[20]

Of the nine authentic *autos* Rojas is known to have written, three have been lost (*Las ferias de Madrid, Sansón,* and *El Sotillo de Madrid*). Of the six surviving *autos,* two are based on scriptural sources (*El rico avariento* and *La viña de Nabot*), one (*El Hércules*) is drawn from classical mythology, and three may be termed "dogmatic" (*Los acreedores del hombre, Galán, valiente y discreto,* and *El gran patio de palacio*). Only four of the *autos* will be given detailed description here.

El rico avariento

Composed for the feast of Corpus Christi of 1640 in Madrid, *El rico avariento* is preserved in two manuscripts (Nos. 15150 and 15266 in the Biblioteca Nacional). There are numerous textual differences between the two manuscripts. The *auto* is based on the parable of Lazarus and the rich man related in Luke xvi. The same parable also served as the subject of two *comedias* which antedate Rojas' work and which he probably knew: Mira de Amescua's *Vida y muerte de San Lázaro,* first printed under the title of *Comedia famosa del Rico avariento* in the collection *Autos sacramentales con cuatro comedias nuevas y sus loas y entremeses* (Madrid, 1655), and Tirso de Molina's *Tanto es lo de más como lo de menos,* first printed in *Doce comedias nuevas del Maestro Tirso de Molina* (Madrid, 1627). Tirso's *comedia* also involves the parable of the prodigal son.

Rojas follows the biblical story closely, but adds a few allegorical characters of his own invention. *Mundo,* who prides himself on being called the "vanity of vanities," elicits the aid of *Avaricia* and *Gula* in bringing out the worst qualities in *Rico.* The latter is saddened by the thought of death, but *Mundo* bolsters his spirits by promising him unlimited wealth. *Caridad* exhorts *Rico* to practice charity toward the poor, but *Avaricia* and *Gula* prevail upon him to refuse. As *Rico* is enjoying a sumptuous banquet, Lázaro, tormented by hunger and sickness (although he thanks God for giving him the fortitude to bear his suffering), arrives to ask for food. Refused, he gathers a few crumbs from the rich man's table but gives them to hungry dogs. Resigned to follow God's will, Lázaro pronounces a soliloquy with the refrain "Salid sin duelo, lágrimas, corriendo," taken from Garcilaso de la Vega's *Egloga primera.*

Stuffed from overeating, *Rico* falls asleep, whereupon *Muerte* comes to claim him. *Lucifer* thanks *Avaricia* and *Gula* for their effective work, then exults over his acquisition of *Rico,* who is shown roasting in hell. His cries attract Abrahán who arrives carrying the deceased Lázaro, but when *Rico* asks for a drop of water, Abrahán replies that his lack of charity has condemned him to eternal torment. As Lázaro goes to enjoy his reward, *Rico* vainly raises his voice against heaven.

El rico avariento scarcely touches upon the eucharistic theme, and there is little sacramental about it. Its allegory is as simple as can be, since *Avaricia* and *Gula* represent *Rico's* predominant traits, while *Caridad* is the salient characteristic of the generous Lázaro. Notwithstanding its simplicity, however, the *auto* has a pronounced dramatic quality because of the opposing natures of the two leading characters. As in *Los trabajos de Tobías* in which Rojas created an effective scene showing the pathos of Tobias' sufferings, so in the *auto* he again captures the pathos of Lázaro's physical misery. It is of interest to note that in the *auto* Tobias is mentioned by name when *Caridad* exhorts *Rico* to follow the example of that holy man.

Galán, valiente y discreto

This *auto* was composed between 1642 and 1646, but no record of its performance has come down to us. It was printed after Rojas' death in the collection *Autos sacramentales, con cuatro comedias nuevas, y sus loas, y entremeses. Primera parte* (Madrid, 1655). The title and the plot were suggested by Mira de Amescua's *comedia, Galán, valiente y discreto,* believed to have been written in 1630.[21]

Princess Arminda (representing Mankind) is courted by two suitors, *Universo* (the frivolous world) and *Astreo* (Satan), who offer her all sorts of culinary fineries. She is about to choose between them when *Inspiración* restrains her, reporting that another suitor has arrived. He is Emanuel (Christ), who promises her only, "Pues yo no la pienso dar/ a comer sino un bocado" (fol. 153 v.). The morsel in question is, of course, the Holy Eucharist. Arminda then decides to choose the suitor who proves himself to be the most "galán, valiente y discreto."

Emanuel is named the most *galán* when he wins a dance competition by demonstrating five movements representing various stages of the Passion of Christ. He also wins the contest for discretion by giving the proper answer to *Inspiración's* question as to what is most necessary for man. The answer: salvation by virtue of a good death. In the tourney to select the most *valiente,* Emanuel defeats *Astreo* and *Universo,* but a new challenger, *Muerte,* succeeds in striking him a mortal blow. Emanuel revives momentarily to overcome *Muerte* before he dies on the cross. Two angels descend to carry the crucified Emanuel to heaven. Although *Galán, valiente y discreto* involves the eucharistic theme and is more ambitious in its use of allegory than *El rico avariento*, it lacks the dramatic impact of the latter. Rojas, like Lope de Vega, was more at ease in adapting biblical episodes to the form of the *auto* than in creating his own allegories.

La viña de Nabot

Preserved in two manuscripts in the Biblioteca Nacional (Nos. 15585 and 17398), *La viña de Nabot* has been edited by Américo Castro.[22] It is not known when it was composed or first performed, but the second manuscript bears the note that it was copied in 1648 for the feast of Corpus Christi in Granada in that year. Since Rojas died in January of 1648, it is unlikely that the *auto* was written specifically for that occasion but probably was written for an earlier celebration in another city, perhaps Madrid.

The nucleus of the plot is provided by III Kings xxi, although a few incidents are taken from other chapters of the same book. Rojas added a few incidents and characters of his own invention. As the *auto* begins, Nabot escorts King Acab into his vineyard, explaining the symbolism of the trees which surround it. Nabot's vineyard workers—*Fe, Esperanza, Caridad*, and *Trabajo*—arrive to partake of the bread and wine awaiting them. The king leaves indignantly when *Trabajo* tells him that he cannot go to heaven without him (that is, without work).

Smitten by the beauty of Jezabel, King Acab proposes to her. Although she is engaged to marry Jeub, she accepts his proposal on the condition that he worship Baal rather than the God of Israel. She then declares her intention of killing all Jewish priests and prophets who refuse to worship her deity. She breaks off with Jeub, whose grief is assuaged by *Fe* and *Esperanza*. Nabot abandons King Acab because he has renounced *Fe*.

The prophet Elías exhorts heaven to punish Acab for worshipping Baal, whereupon an angel appears to tell him that his prayers will be answered: it will not rain in Samaria until he requests it. Meanwhile, the angel brings eucharistic bread to sustain Elías and other faithful Jews. Later, Elías journeys to Samaria where the drought has laid waste to the fields and flocks. Jezabel orders a sacrifice to Baal to bring rain but to no avail. Elías invokes God's wrath on the idol which is overturned in an earthquake. At the prophet's request, it begins to rain; but Jezabel remains steadfast in her devotion to Baal, swearing to kill all the Jews.

Following the biblical account, King Acab repents momentarily for his misdeeds. He desires to purchase Nabot's vineyard or trade him for it, but Nabot refuses to part with it. Jezabel then resolves to take revenge on Nabot, who is stoned to death by *Ira* and *Soberbia*. Upon Elías' request, heaven destroys Acab with fire. Jeub, now King of Israel, returns to punish Jezabel. Still faithful to Baal, she commits suicide by jumping off a cliff.

Elías invites Jeub to enter Nabot's vineyard, not to possess it but only to enjoy it. Sacramental bread and wine await Jeub and his followers. Elías ascends to heaven in a chariot of fire, leaving *Fe, Esperanza,* and *Caridad* to accompany Jeub.

Although *La viña de Nabot* is noteworthy among Rojas' *autos* for the prominence of the eucharistic theme, its chief interest resides in the role of Jezabel, whose fierce pride and vengeful nature provide most of the drama. She resembles Medea and Rosimunda and the other headstrong females of Rojas' secular plays.

El gran patio de palacio

As mentioned in Chapter 1, this *auto sacramental* is, as far as it is known, the last thing that Rojas ever wrote. It was composed for the Corpus Christi festival in Madrid in 1647 when permission was unexpectedly given to hold the festival, although the country was still officially in mourning because of the death of Prince Baltasar Carlos in October of the preceding year. As remarked earlier, Jerónimo Cáncer states in his *loa sacramental* which precedes Rojas' *auto* that Rojas wrote it in three days, "which is a good excuse if by chance it is not good."

Although the *auto* is not especially good, it, nevertheless, is of interest. It contains numerous autobiographical references, and, at the same time, reveals a nasty snobbishness not found in

Rojas' earlier works. The *patio* in the title symbolizes the world and also, whether Rojas intended it or not, the court of Philip IV. This is not to say, of course, that the entire *auto* should be read on two levels.

Guided by *Ignorancia* and *Noticia, Hombre* goes to the king's palace where he intends to bring a suit against his brother *Mayorazgo* (Christ) who, he claims, was charged by their father to give him sustenance. After seeing a document in which *Mayorazgo* promised to give man the "true bread," *Custodio* agrees that *Mayorazgo* has obligated himself to *Hombre* although he refuses to present the latter's demand. *Cautela,* however, agrees to do so. Apprised of *Hombre's* claim, *Mayorazgo* invites him to his table, but *Hombre* rejects the invitation, not wanting to surrender his freedom. *Hombre* then decides to ask the Supreme Tribunal for justice.

When Prince Lucero (Satan) learns of *Hombre's* legal suit, he resolves to obstruct the making of the bread. He then calls on *Hermosura* and *Vanidad* to divert *Hombre's* attention. *Inspiración* informs *Hombre* of the counter charges brought against him by *Mayorazgo,* but absorbed in his pleasure, *Hombre* insists that there is ample time to answer the charges. Later *Inspiración* returns with *Custodio* who serves a final warning on *Hombre,* advising him to seek the intercession of his brother's *Esposa* (the Church) in order to avoid condemnation. *Hombre* confesses to *Sacerdocio,* a special judge of the Supreme Tribunal, that he owes his life to his brother who, moreover, has sustained him. *Sacerdocio* then absolves *Hombre* of the charges against him. At the end of the *auto, Mayorazgo* invites him to his chapel which is

En mi Palacio; aquí tengo
los alimentos que darte,
mi Capilla es el granero
del mejor Pan.

(In my palace; here I have
nourishment to give you,
for my chapel is the granary
of the best Bread.

HOMBRE:

        ¿Dónde está
este Pan?

                 Where is
this Bread?

MAYOR:

      Este es mi cuerpo . . .

            This is my body . . .

MUSICOS:

> A *la mesa del Pan* [Let's go] to the table
> *que de valde, de valde lo* where the Bread is given free.)
> *dan.*[23]

El gran patio de palacio is obviously one of the most allegorical of Rojas' *autos,* and although Valbuena Prat finds the allegory "coarse and common," it shows that Rojas was learning to work adequately, if not skillfully, in a genre alien to him.

CHAPTER 6

The Novelistic Plays

FIVE of Rojas' plays may be classified as novelistic, although only three of them can be definitely traced to fictional sources. *Persiles y Segismunda* (Rojas' spelling) dramatizes a few episodes of Cervantes' posthumous Byzantine novel, *Persiles y Sigismunda* (1617). *Los bandos de Verona* is a melodramatic version of the story of Romeo and Juliet, and derives from an Italian novella. *Los celos de Rodamonte* is an uninspired dramatization of various episodes of Ludovico Ariosto's romantic epic, *Orlando furioso*. Perhaps it would be more accurate to call Rojas' play a *comedia caballeresca* in view of the chivalric background of its characters and subject matter.

El primer Marqués de Astorga, which has never been printed, is principally concerned with the efforts of Alvar Pérez Osorio to redeem his good name on the battlefield against the Moors. It can properly be called a novelistic play not only because of the nature and treatment of its plot, but also because it involves a variation of the central episode of the anonymous Moorish novel, *Historia del Abencerraje y la hermosa Jarifa. El desafío de Carlos Quinto* presents a different case. It is a historical play in that the proposed duel between the Christian emperor and the sultan of Turkey was actually a matter of international concern (although it never took place), but its historicity is so diluted by extraneous incidents that it smacks more of fiction than of truth.

As a group the novelistic plays are the least rewarding in Rojas' entire production. They are essentially wild melodramas which utilize every striking *coup de théâtre* known to the dramatist, but for all their intrigue and hair-raising adventure, they make poor dramatic literature. Perhaps like many other Golden

Age plays they would be more effective on the stage than as reading fare.

I *Persiles y Segismunda*

Rojas' dramatization of Cervantes' Byzantine novel is his earliest individual play that can be dated with some certainty, although it is probable that he wrote other plays before it. It was performed on February 23, 1633, before the king and queen at the palace El Pardo, and was later included in the *Primera parte* of 1640. Cervantes' novel (which he confidently expected would crown his career as a writer) has been roundly criticized for its shapeless plot, excessive action, innumerable transitory characters, and lack of focus. It simply suffers from too many people, places, and incidents. If this is true of the novel, any attempt to adapt it to the more confining form of the drama would seem to be doomed to failure. Rojas' play is certainly an artistic failure, but its frenzied action and savage characters mark it as a monument in the history of melodrama. The play is of interest only because of its action, its melodramatic devices, and its violence.

Having searched for each other for six years, during which time they have had countless reunions and separations, Persiles and Segismunda finally wash ashore—separately—on the island of Tile (Thule) where the barbarous chieftain Bradamiro intends to sacrifice them in order to carry out his father's testament for selecting a new king: he who eats of Christian hearts with no signs of revulsion is to rule on Thule. When some of Bradamiro's women warriors refuse to pierce the bodies of the helpless captives with arrows, a fight breaks out. Persiles manages to cut his bonds—and his wrists—then frees his fellow captive (Segismunda), whom he does not recognize because she is disguised as a man. They escape together but become separated in a forest which is set ablaze by Bradamiro, who then goes to butcher the Christian captives imprisoned in a dungeon. Seeing him approach, Segismunda hides in an anchored boat, but fearing the Christians may escape in it, Bradamiro cuts the boat adrift. As the fire edges nearer, Tarimón, a Christian captive disguised as a barbarian, takes advantage of Bradamiro's distraction to release the captives, then locks the savage in the dungeon where he stones him before the fire can do its work. By this time, Persiles realizes that his fellow captive was indeed Segismunda, but when he calls out to her he can barely hear her faint reply because the boat has drifted out to sea.

The second act is much tamer. In Dalmatia, where the hapless Segismunda was washed ashore, King Leopoldo has fallen in love with her but she remains unresponsive. Leopoldo's sister, a princess but no lady, advises him to rape her, but he is too much of a gentleman to do so. At this point, the *infanta's* fiancé, the prince of Transylvania from whom she has not heard in six years, arrives to claim his bride. He is in reality Persiles, who came only because he heard Segismunda was there. The lovers make plans to flee, but that very night a plot against the king breaks out. The king emerges unscathed from a shotgun blast, but as Segismunda and Persiles are preparing to board their escape ship, Persiles is apprehended with a smoking shotgun in his possession. Although he denies any complicity in the plot against the king's life, he confesses his love for Segismunda and his plan to abduct her. They are imprisoned.

In Act III, moved by an account of the couple's many misfortunes, the king is about to release them when Tarimón brings the news that an army headed by Persiles' brother and Segismunda's father, king of Balachia, is coming to liberate them. King Leopoldo resolves to resist the invaders. Meanwhile, wishing to see her sweetheart who is being held in solitary confinement, Segismunda makes her way with a light to the castle wall near the prison tower. Hearing her cries, Persiles issues from the tower and edges toward her, but the light goes out causing him to make a misstep. Segismunda grabs his hand as he falls, plunging to the earth with him. Mortally wounded, the ill-starred lovers manage to crawl to each other and die hand-in-hand. Tarimón then confesses that he, ironically, invented the report of the invading army to frighten Leopoldo into releasing the victims.

Although this early play has about it a maladroitness of technique (especially the long soliloquies used more for expository than lyrical purposes, and the clumsy dialogue which paralyzes the action as the lovers recount their infinite adversities), it is important in tracing Rojas' development because, as previously remarked, it anticipates one of the most persistent and distinctive traits of his dramaturgy: the violent death which not only claims ruthless villains but which also overtakes the virtuous. In this same chapter we shall also consider *Los bandos de Verona*, Rojas' version of the tale of Romeo and Juliet, in which he, following the conclusion of Lope de Vega's play on the same subject, reverses his general tendency by bringing the young lovers to a happy end. But to my knowledge, in his *Persiles*, Rojas is the only dramatist of his day who willfully violates his source by changing a happy ending to a tragic one.

II   *Los celos de Rodamonte*

Published in Rojas' *Primera parte* of 1640, *Los celos de Rodamonte* is based on various episodes of Ariosto's *Orlando furioso*. Perhaps Rojas also knew Lope de Vega's earlier play of the same title, the sources of which have been studied by Menéndez Pelayo.[1] The Spanish critic could usually find something good to say about most of Lope's plays but he wasted few words on this one: "This play is one of the worst and most monstruous of its kind."[2] Nor was he any more appreciative of Rojas' play which he found "no better."[3]

Los celos de Rodamonte begins auspiciously when Doralice, brought to France to meet her fiancé Rodamonte, pronounces a lovely soliloquy, an apostrophe to dawn. But having taken one look at Rodamonte, whose violent manner terrifies her, Doralice dreads being left alone with him when her father, King Agricán, returns to Granada. Consequently, she spends the rest of the play, often in the company of Mandricardo with whom she falls in love, trying to elude him. Mandricardo, meanwhile, seeks to avenge himself on Roldán (Orlando), who killed his brother, and Reynaldos, who seduced his sister. Duels, battles, magic spells, sleeping potions, and whatnot follow in rapid order. Finally, when Rodamonte, insanely jealous of Doralice, sees her escape with her lover from a fire he prepared to destroy them, he drops dead—more of apoplexy than from the wounds inflicted upon him by Roldán.

Perhaps Rojas was trying to outdo Ariosto in his raillery against the unreality of the chivalric ideal, but raillery or not, it is a very bad play. It does, however, have a lively *gracioso,* Baraúnda (Noise), whose satire of foreign nationals is evident in the following free translation:

> You may think I'm just a bum,   19
> But one thing I'll tell you, chum:
> I've learned the ways of foreign men,
> Nary a trick has slipped my ken.
> When I meet Frenchmen on the street,
> I hold my hat and seek retreat.
> Whenever I see a German come,
> I put lock and key to my beer and rum.
> With Genoese I become a phoney,
> With Sicilians, slick as macaroni.
> Around Portuguese I swallow my purse,
> Those thievin' rascals would rob a hearse.
> But around Italians, this I entreat,
> Give me a corset to protect my seat.
> (Ed. 1640, Act III, fol. 183 r.)

III   *El desafío de Carlos Quinto*

Preserved in an undated *suelta* and reprinted in Mesonero Romanos' collection of Rojas' plays in the *Biblioteca de Autores Españoles,* this is probably the play performed in the Royal Palace on May 28, 1635 with the title of *El desafío del emperador.*[4] It treats the same subject as a play attributed, perhaps erroneously, to Lope de Vega, entitled *El cerco de Viena y socorro por Carlos V.*[5] It is difficult to say whether Rojas knew the earlier play, but whether he did or not, he did little to improve upon it. So bad is Rojas' play, in fact, that Cotarelo wanted to absolve him of the responsibility of having composed it.[6] There are, however, no grounds for questioning his authorship. The versification, several of the dramatic situations, and the comic subplot are typical of him.

The historical sections of the play concern the siege of Vienna in 1532 by Solimán (Suleiman the Magnificent), sultan of Turkey, who supported the claims of Juan Sepusio Baiboda (John Zapolya) to the throne of Hungary against Don Fernando, brother of Carlos V. The main conflict centers upon a challenge issued by Solimán to Carlos to settle the war by a personal duel. Will Carlos accept the challenge or no? After much consultation and debate with his followers, he does. Confronted by Carlos' acceptance of his challenge, will Solimán have courage enough to go through with the duel or will he quail at the prospect of facing the redoubtable emperor? The answer to this question is not forthcoming until the final scene. Only then do we learn from Juan Sepusio, who comes to beg for the emperor's forgiveness, that Solimán deserted him and fled the field.

There is one serious attempt to explore character: a soliloquy in the form of a prayer in which Carlos' fine Christian idealism shines through. This is not enough to sustain interest, and for that reason Rojas tried to beef up the play by including a romantic subplot (in which there is much talk about the conflicting demands of love and duty) and by including a comic subplot. The humor is bizarre, even for Rojas. The comic subplot involves a Galician soldier-lackey, Buscaruido, (Noise Seeker) who is constantly pursued by an amorous hermaphrodite, Mari Bernardo, "A name both male and female/ very much a woman in her stubbornness/ and very much a man in experience." (BAE, I, 409b) At the end of the play, Buscaruido decides to marry this "compound of two species" since that is the only way "she" will leave him alone.

When his material ran thin or he did not know what to do with it, Rojas frequently resorted to freakishness; but not even an amorous hermaphrodite could do much to enliven *El desafío de Carlos Quinto.*

IV *El primer Marqués de Astorga*

With its tale of lovers' woes set against a background of fighting between Christians and Moors, *El primer Marqués de Astorga* is a pleasant play of little consequence. Rojas did not see fit to include it in the two volumes of his plays which he compiled for publication, and it has never been printed. Two manuscript copies survive.[7]

Accused by Don Nuño de Aguirre of conspiring against King Enrique III (el Doliente) of Castile, Alvar Pérez Osorio is obliged to leave his sweetheart, Blanca, in the clutches of his rival as he goes to vindicate himself on the battlefield. Blanca pleads with Osorio to take her with him, a request that he refuses on the grounds that such conduct would bring dishonor to them both. Unmindful of her reputation (as are many of Rojas' heroines), Blanca remains unconvinced. After Osorio has regained the king's favor by capturing Archidona and Alora, Blanca, disguised as a man, tracks him down. She is accompanied by Rosana, a Moorish girl who is also in pursuit of her man, Don Diego de Velasco, whose escape from captivity she arranged on the condition that he would return to her. Both pairs of lovers, not surprisingly, are reconciled. The king dowers Rosana, who becomes a Christian, and bestows on Osorio the title of Marqués de Astorga.

With its mixture of romantic intrigue and border wars, its variation of the Abencerraje story, and its women disguised as men in order to rejoin their lovers, Rojas' play is similar to dozens of others of the Golden Age. Perhaps its most distinctive feature is its poetry, especially the exquisite love lyrics. Cotarelo, basing his opinion on notes found on the manuscript in the Biblioteca Nacional, suggested that the play was privately performed by laymen.[8] Certainly it is an appropriate play for courtiers to perform, since the roles make no excessive demands upon the talents of the actors, and there is ample opportunity for gentlemen and ladies to recite graceful poetry to each other.

V Los Bandos de Verona

Commissioned to write a play for the inauguration of the new coliseum in the park of Buen Retiro, Rojas chose to dramatize the story of Romeo and Juliet. Its presentation on February 4, 1640, marks the last date for which information is available concerning the first performance of any of his plays, other than the *autos sacramentales*. One would like to think, however, that it is not the last secular play he wrote because *Los bandos de Verona* is one of his most disappointing plays.

Rojas' play is one of three extant seventeenth-century Spanish *comedias* based on Romeo and Juliet, the other two being Lope de Vega's *Castelvines y Monteses* (probably composed between 1606 and 1612)[9] and Cristóbal de Rozas' *Los amante de Verona* (printed in 1666). According to Cotarelo, the sources of Rojas' drama are Luigi da Porta's *Giulietta* (c. 1530) and a novella by Masuccio Salernitano,[10] but I see no reason for assuming that he did not also know Matteo Bandello's novella which served as Lope's source and probably Cristóbal de Rozas' as well.[11] One thing seems certain, however: although Lope's play was first printed in 1647, several years after *Los bandos de Verona* was written, Rojas must have been familiar with it. Similarities in detail between the two plays are few, but two or three scenes in Rojas' melodrama seem to have been suggested by Lope's play.

The most obvious similarity between them, in their departure from their sources, is their happy endings. Of greater consequence is the fact that both plays have been held up as examples illustrating the principle of poetic justice, a principle of paramount importance in the moral attitude of Spanish dramatists toward their art. A. A. Parker, who has so ably interpreted that attitude, has this to say about the application of the principle of poetic justice in the two plays:

Just as the principle of poetic justice can deprive a Spanish comedy of a happy ending, so can it steer a tragic story away from a tragic end. The story of Romeo and Juliet offers an illustration . . . In Shakespeare's version of the story the tragedy is generally held to lie in the fact that the lovers are sacrificial victims: if the family feud is to end and peace come to Verona it shall come about through the deaths of the two luckless martyrs of love. Such a conception of tragedy as the sacrifice of innocent victims who, on the level of the action, find their deaths through an unhappy mischance, is impossible in the Spanish drama because there is no justice in it. Spanish dramatists present no victims of destiny or mischance, but only of wrongdoing—their own, or someone else's. The principle of poetic justice required not only that the guilty should suffer but also that there should be no innocent victim . . . That is why, when the same story of Romeo and Juliet that served Shakespeare served Spanish dramatists also, it was given a happy ending, and the innocent lovers allowed, after the trials of a persecuting fate, to enjoy the reward of their love. So Lope in *Castelvines y Monteses* and Rojas Zorrilla in *Los bandos de Verona*—plays that have been adduced to support the contention that the Spanish drama has little conception of tragedy.[12]

It is ironical, indeed, that Rojas' dramatization of the tragic tale of Romeo and Juliet can be held up as an example of a play illustrating Spanish dramatists' fondness for fabricating a happy ending, in violation of their sources, for the sole reason that such an ending serves to provide poetic justice. Although Rojas tended to mete out poetic justice to his characters, he was equally prone to end his plays with spectacular death scenes whether justice was served or not, as seen in *Persiles y Segismunda*. It should be pointed out too that Cristóbal de Rozas (although he confused the Montagues and Capulets of Verona with the feuding Florentine families of the Guelphs and Ghibellines) felt no compulsion in *Los amantes de Verona* to avoid the death of the lovers. Their sacrifice, as in Shakespeare's tragedy, presumably serves a larger justice by bringing peace to strife-torn Verona. We shall probably never know why Rojas chose to follow Lope's example.

But what makes Rojas' play a disappointing one, even an outrageous one, is not so much the happy ending but his treatment of the rest of the tale. Absent is the balcony scene of Shakespeare, absent are the lovely lyrical exchanges of the lovers (poetry which Rojas *could* write so well), absent are the pathos and grief of Romeo and Juliet victimized by their own families. On the other hand, Rojas complicated an already busy plot in many ways. Julia's father insists that she marry one of her kinsman, either her cousin Andrés or Count Paris, who is married to Alejandro Romeo's (Romeo's) sister but from whom he seeks an annulment on the grounds that she was forced by her family to marry him against her will. When Julia admits she loves Alejandro and refuses to marry anyone else, her father gives her the choice of dying by the knife or by poison. Not wanting her father to disgrace himself by killing her, she gulps the poison. Grief-stricken, Don Antonio then reveals that he had not intended to kill his daughter but merely to threaten her. He does not know, of course, that the poison is really a sleeping potion. The contest of wills between father and daughter over the choice of her husband-to-be (a conflict that figures in so many of Rojas' plays) provides the most dramatic moment of the action.

Again taking a lead from Lope de Vega, Rojas exploits to the utmost both the melodramatic and the comical possibilities of the scene in the burial vaults of San Carlos Church where Alejandro Romeo, accompanied by his trembling servant, goes to mourn his "deceased" sweetheart. While the *gracioso* almost dies of fright, Julia is revived; but the lovers are again separated when the lights go out and Julia falls into the hands of her amorous cousin, Andrés, who later attempts to rape her. Now believing Julia to be dead, Alejandro decides to take revenge on the Capulets by destroying with artillery the castle in which they have taken refuge. Various persons appear individually on the castle wall to ask Alejandro to call off the siege: Don Antonio, Count Paris, his sister Elena, his cousin Carlos, a prisoner of the Capulets, but he ignores their pleas. Finally, Don Antonio sends Julia herself to plead for the deliverance of the innocent people in the castle. After recovering from his surprise at finding her alive, Alejandro agrees—on the condition that Don Antonio will permit him to marry Julia and that Count Paris will take Elena back. Both will.

Perhaps the people who crowded into the new coliseum of the Buen Retiro to see *Los bandos de Verona* liked the melodrama, but those who like Shakespeare's *Romeo and Juliet* cannot help feeling defrauded.

CHAPTER 7

The Cape-and-Sword Plays

LIKE most Spanish dramatists of his age, Rojas wrote several *comedias de capa y espada* which had become the regular bill of fare of the Spanish theater during the career of Lope de Vega, although their invention is sometimes credited to Diego Jiménez de Enciso.[1] Their name derives from the cloak and sword worn by men of the upper classes as part of their dress. Rennert has defined these *comedias* as "plays that are based upon events and occurrences in ordinary daily life and in which no higher personages intervene than noblemen or gentlemen, and which are acted in the ordinary costume of the time."[2] One can only say that if it were true that these plays reflect the "ordinary daily life" of Spanish society in the seventeenth century, theirs was a frenetic existence indeed. Some of them do contain candid portraits of Spanish manners and customs, especially in Madrid, but they tend to emphasize not the ordinary but the unusual. For this reason, I have distinguished between them and Rojas' comedies of customs which are more deeply rooted in the reality of Spanish life, although they too are not lacking in intrigue.

The cape-and-sword plays are essentially romantic comedies in which the usual boy-meets-girl formula is attended by all the hazards presented by the Spanish code of honor, although a happy ending can be expected because conjugal honor is not involved. Seldom, however, have lovers of any time or place had a more difficult time. They must contend with their own jealousies and misunderstandings; they are constantly pursued by unwelcome admirers of the opposite sex; they must scheme to see each other in secrecy to avoid the watchful eyes of the girl's father or brother who are ever alert to punish those who transgress upon their honor. As a consequence, ruses and intrigue of

all kinds—disguises, mistaken identities, eavesdropping, intercepted letters, etc.—are the regular stock-in-trade of the genre.

Not only do the cape-and-sword plays depend upon conventional devices to produce excitement and provide suspense but
they also employ a number of characters whose roles are largely
stereotyped.[3] Most of these stock characters—*galán, dama, criado,
criada, hermano,* and *contracriado*—are found as early as 1517
when they appear in Bartolomé de Torres Naharro's *Comedia
Himenea,* which has been called the first *comedia de capa y
espada.* Although Lope de Vega and his contemporaries did
not alter greatly their basic roles, they complicated the intrigue
by increasing the number of such characters, especially the
gallants and the women who become rivals in contests of love.[4]

In view of their repetitious plots and stereotyped characters,
it is not surprising that most foreign critics, as well as many
Spaniards, especially eighteenth-century neoclassicists, condemned the *comedias de capa y espada* for being like so many
bullets made in the same mold. The most talented Golden Age
dramatists, however, were able to work within their conventional
framework and still produce plays of considerable originality
and merit. Rojas was one of them.

Six of Rojas' plays conform on all, or most, counts to the
characteristic pattern of cape-and-sword plays: *Donde hay agravios no hay celos, No hay amigo para amigo, No hay duelo entre
dos amigos, Obligados y ofendidos, y gorrón de Salamanca,
Primero es la honra que el gusto,* and *Sin honra no hay amistad.*
The first two have been widely praised for their overall excellence, but their chief interest lies in the response of their
graciosos to the demands of the honor code. The *gracioso's*
renunciation of honor is frequent in earlier Spanish drama, but
it is unlikely that any other dramatist went as far as Rojas in
exploiting the humor to be gained by the servant's repudiation
of a system of values which endangered his life and comfort.
Since Rojas reacted strongly against the conventional treatment
of honor in his serious dramas, it is no wonder that he seized
the opportunity of poking fun at the honor code in his comedies.

Primero es la honra que el gusto and *No hay duelo entre dos
amigos* are run-of-the-mill plays about which I shall have little
to say, although it should be noted that, strictly speaking, the

latter is not a true cape-and-sword play in that the action takes place at the French court and its lovers are persons of royalty and the upper nobility. Its basic motives and its intrigue are, however, typical of the genre.

I Donde hay agravios no hay celos

One of Rojas' most popular plays, Donde hay agravios (printed in 1640) enjoyed a brief revival in the eighteenth century and again in the nineteenth century when it was recast in five acts by Juan Eugenio Hartzenbusch with the title El amo criado (1841). It is occasionally performed today. It was also adapted for the French stage by Paul Scarron with the title Jodolet ou le maître valet (first performed in 1643, printed in 1645). Scarron's adaptation served in turn as the model of William D'Avenant's The Man's the Master (1669). What attracted the attention of both the French and English playwrights was the device, introduced by Rojas,[5] of having master and servant exchange roles, a device permitting many comical incongruities as the swaggering lackey takes pleasure in outraging his new peers, men and women alike. Molière employed the same device in one of his earliest masterpieces, Les précieuses ridicules (1659).

The complicated plot is skillfully developed. Don Juan de Alvarado comes to Madrid on two missions: to find the man who seduced his sister Ana and killed his brother, and to locate the home of his fiancée, Doña Inés de Rojas, whom he has never seen. Arriving at night, he is startled to see a man jump from the balcony of his fiancée's home. Suspecting that the man is her lover, he changes clothes and names with his servant Sancho in order to determine the relationship between them. This he is able to do because Sancho had mistakenly sent Inés his own portrait instead of his master's. The boorish conduct of the feigned Don Juan soon disgusts Doña Inés and her father, Don Fernando, while the pretended valet wins the affection of Inés and her servant Beatriz.

Doña Ana arrives at Don Fernando's home, confiding in him as a former friend of her dead father that she yielded to a man who killed one of her brothers and then deserted her. After pledging her his protection, Don Fernando discovers that her faithless lover is his nephew, Don Lope de Rojas, who has recently sought the hand of Inés, and who, admitted into her room by Beatriz, escaped by means of the balcony just in time to be seen by Don Juan. After Ana discovers the presence of her lover and her brother, Don Fernando insists that Sancho, still posing as his master, avenge his honor on Don Lope. Sancho wants no part of a duel, but relying on assistance from his master, agrees to meet Don Lope in a room of the house. Don Juan is obliged to come to Sancho's rescue, admits who he is, and challenges Don Lope. The latter agrees to rectify his offense against Doña Ana by marrying her. Doña Inés gives her hand to Don Juan, and Sancho announces that he will marry Beatriz.

Donde hay agravios no hay celos has been praised by many critics, both Spanish and foreign, but none has been more enthusiastic about it than the nineteenth-century historian of the Spanish theater, Adolph F. von Schack, who considered it to be the best of Rojas' comedies because of its well-ordered plot, excellent characterization, and superbly designed situations, calculated to enhance its comic effect.[6] There is no doubt that the play contains some of Rojas' most skillful dramatic writing, but it is, after all, to the rollicking humor resulting from the exchange of roles of master and servant that it owes most of its appeal. Many plays exploit the *gracioso's* cowardice for comic effect, but Rojas could have employed no better device than the exchange of roles to show the different attitudes of *galán* and *gracioso* toward the point of honor. When poor Sancho finds himself confronted with a duel which he had not bargained for, he engages in a soliloquy in which he muses on the absurdity of the honor code and the folly of duelling:

> Duelist, weighted down
> with the point of honor,
> tell me, fool, is it not worse
> to be dead than slapped? . . .
> It seems that the living
> do not know what it is to be dead.
> (*BAE*, III, 163a)

By the very nature of its plot, *Donde hay agravios* necessarily involves a more prominent role for the *gracioso* than had formerly been the case in most Spanish plays, but after its success, not only Rojas but also his younger contemporaries, especially Agustín Moreto, continued to give greater prominence to the lackey. Also, Rojas' *graciosas*, who shared something of the blatant feminism of their mistresses, were not content to have their roles subordinated to those of the male servants. For this reason Beatriz, who finds herself temporarily idle in the play, insists upon her right to pronounce a soliloquy:

> I alone have no one
> to tell my troubles to;
> well, here goes a soliloquy,
> although I have never seen
> women servants in other plays
> go so far as to soliloquize.
> (*BAE,* III, 165c)

Donde hay agravios no hay celos is perhaps Rojas' first play in which his penchant for burlesque is sustained throughout most of the three acts, as Sancho apes the manners of middle-class Madrilenian society. In his future comedies burlesque becomes a constant ingredient.

II *No hay amigo para amigo*

Also printed in the *Primera parte* of Rojas' plays, *No hay amigo para amigo* is a play of complicated intrigue center-ing upon problems of honor, love, and friendship. Back in Madrid after a long absence in Flanders, Don Luis Pacheco looks up his former comrade in arms, Don Lope de Castro whose help he needs because his life is threatened by Don Alonso, whose brother he killed in a duel. To make matters worse, Don Luis is now in love with Aurora, Alonso's sister who knows him by the name of Carlos. The lovers cannot meet fo obvious reasons. Furthermore, Alonso is in love with Estrella former sweetheart of Luis who abandoned her for Aurora, al though Estrella continues to prefer Luis. Don Lope, unawar that Luis is the man who killed Alonso's brother, promises t aid both men.

After many complications arising from these confused rel

tionships, Don Lope discovers that his two friends who sought his help are enemies and that a duel between them is inevitable. He refuses to side with either one since he is obligated to both, but he insists on a fair fight. When the duel begins, Luis falls but Alonso refuses to take advantage of him. At this point, Don Lope intervenes, persuading Alonso that "to pardon is to conquer." Alonso is glad to accept Luis as his brother-in-law when he learns that he loves Aurora instead of Estrella. The latter, realizing that she can never win Luis, settles for Alonso.

As demonstrated by the resolution of the plot, *No hay amigo para amigo* makes the point that when a man, such as Don Lope, promises to help others he is honor-bound to protect them even if they are in the wrong. However, as the title suggests, if he is equally obligated to two men who are sworn enemies, such as Don Luis and Don Alonso, he must see to it that one does not take unfair advantage of the other because his own honor is at stake. Thus it is that at one point in the play, when Don Lope is denounced in turn by the two men whom he promised to befriend because of his refusal to side with one against the other, he is put in the position, temporarily at least, of facing a duel with both his friends. We can only conclude that friendship was put to a severe test by the many ramifications of the honor code.

Interspersed throughout Acts II and III is a comic subplot which has little to do with the main plot although it also involves a point of honor and a duel that never comes off. When Fernando, servant of Don Luis, asks Moscón, servant of Don Lope, where the latter lives, Moscón answers him impudently. Fernando slaps him. Moscón admits that the blow angered him a bit, but when Fernando asserts that he will defend his act, Moscón refuses to take offense because he did not really feel the blow. On learning that his servant had not avenged his outraged honor, Don Lope questions him indignantly:

DON LOPE:
> When he gave you the blow,
> what did you do?

MOSCÓN:
> Receive it.

DON LOPE:

> In short, didn't you seek satisfaction?
> When he gave you the blow,
> did you face up to him?

MOSCON:

> Face up to him, no,
> because he "unfaced" me first . . .

DON LOPE:

> Don't you even have enough courage
> to avenge yourself with his death? . . .

MOSCON:

> Let me ask, since you know about these things:
> if through courage or by luck
> he should kill me,
> who would be better off?
> (*BAE*, III, 95c)

Moscón may reason out of fear but it is difficult to argue with his logic. Finally, persuaded by his master that he must avenge his honor, he sends a challenge to Fernando, then comes on stage to wait for his opponent and to practice fencing. But first, rosary in hand, he remembers to pray for his victim-to-be. As he continues his soliloquy (Rojas' *graciosos* love to soliloquize as much as Hamlet), he begins to muse upon the vulnerability of the human body. After enumerating more than twenty sensitive parts of the anatomy, including "thirty yards of intestines," Moscón momentarily loses his nerve, but he shakes off his fear, bracing himself by enacting an imaginary duel with Fernando in which he defeats his enemy. He addresses these words to his "victim" just as Fernando arrives to overhear him:

> Go say your prayers.
> I say there is no use in begging
> or in kneeling before me;
> die, Fernando, you coward.
> (*BÁE*, III, 99a)

Fernando confronts Moscón with the written challenge and makes him read it aloud. It is a masterpiece of cowardly candor and a beautiful parody of the formal challenges issued by gentle men of the upper classes to their adversaries. It is signed, "Your best friend, Moscón." After Moscón disclaims authorship of the challenge, Fernando gives him a drubbing and calls him "chicken" (*gallina*). Moscón does not dispute the appropriateness of the term but takes solace in the fact that he complied with his honor by having the courage to "meet" his foe on the duelling field.

It was an irony of fate that Rojas, who loved to jest at the code of honor in general and at duelling in particular, almost lost his life in 1638 (if contemporary conjecture is correct) as the result of a duel.

Paul Scarron, leading dramatist of the burlesque movement in France in the 1640's, not only adapted Rojas' *Donde hay agravios no hay celos* for the French stage but also based his second play on Spanish sources. For *Les trois Dorothées ou le Jodolet soufleté* (performed in 1646 but rewritten and renamed *Le Jodolet duelliste* in 1651), he borrowed seventeen scenes from Tirso de Molina's *No hay peor sordo*, three scenes from Rojas' *La traición busca el castigo*, and seven scenes from the comic subplot of *No hay amigo para amigo*. These scenes, concerning the enmity and "duel" of the lackeys, are precisely those which led Scarron to change the title of his play to *Le Jodolet duelliste*.[7]

III *No hay duelo entre dos amigos*

This play, called by Cotarelo "an excellent *comedia* of intrigue and characters,"[8] is preserved in two different undated *sueltas* of the seventeenth century, both of which bear Rojas' name as the author. I have treated it as his because there is no evidence to the contrary, but I am not convinced that he wrote it in its entirety. Only the second act seems characteristic of his versification and style. Perhaps the first and third acts were written by collaborators.

The play is of interest only because of its plot which, although trite, is skillfully worked out. Count Carlos and the Duke of Guisa are great friends but they apparently keep from one another the secrets of their hearts. The count is in love with Princess Isabela, but the king wants her to marry the duke. The latter is in love with Leonor de Valois, who prefers Carlos. Isabela also prefers Carlos but suspects that he loves Leonor.

Carlos thinks that the duke is in love with Isabela, while the duke believes that his friend loves Leonor. Both men suspect each other of disloyalty, but so great is their friendship that each volunteers to go into exile because he would have no alternative but to settle his differences by a duel if he remained. Finally the two friends learn that each was sacrificing his true love because of friendship, but by this time the king, understandably out of patience, commands the duke to marry Isabela and Carlos to marry Leonor. The duke takes the king aside and explains the mix-up which threatened his friendship with Carlos, but although the king is sympathetic, he does not think it would be fitting for him to rescind his orders. He purposefully makes a slip of the tongue, however, ordering the duke to give his hand to Leonor; and he can do no less than make another slip and order Carlos to marry Isabela.

Rojas would not be greatly grieved if this play were incorrectly excised from his production.

IV   *Obligados y ofendidos, y gorrón de Salamanca*

One of Roja's most delightful comedies, *Obligados y ofendidos* was published twice in 1640, in *Parte 32* of *Comedias de diferentes autores* (Zaragoza) and in the *Primera parte* of Rojas' plays. If, however, it is the play designated by the title *Obligar por defender,* recorded as having been performed in the Royal Palace on June 6, 1631 (perhaps an error for 1635)[9] by the troupe of Juan Martínez de los Ríos, it is one of Rojas' earliest plays. I personally regard it as one of his later and more mature plays.

No precise source for the play has been discovered, although its plot is rather similar in general outline to Guillén de Castro's (?) *Las canas en el papel y dudoso en la venganza*[10] and to Rojas' own *Sin honra no hay amistad.* There are, moreover, other similarities between Rojas' two plays. Unlike most of his cape-and-sword plays, whose action is laid in Madrid, *Sin honra* takes place in Salamanca, and one of its principal characters, Antonio, is a university student, as is the *gracioso* Sabañón. The action of *Obligados y ofendidos* takes place in Toledo, but its principal character is a student who is truant from the University of Salamanca. Crispinillo, the *gracioso,* is also a university student, and like Sabañón, is given to showing off his Latin at every opportunity. There are also certain thematic similarities which will be mentioned later. It is not known which play was written first, but the general similarities in plot and the few similarities in detail suggest that they were composed about the same time.

Various other works probably influenced portions of Rojas' play. The description of student life at Salamanca is reminiscent of scenes at the University of Alcalá in Francisco de Quevedo's *Historia de la vida del Buscón;* and Rojas' colorful gang of professional thugs owes much of its picturesqueness of manner and language to Monipodio and his crew in Cervantes' *Rinconete y Cortadillo.* Rojas probably drew upon Juan Hidalgo's *Romances de germanía* for his vocabulary of thieves' slang, and possibly upon Cubillo de Aragón's *Añasco de Talavera* for his jail scenes. But no matter how much Rojas borrowed from these and other works of underworld life, his play retains a distinctively original flavor.

The play begins in Toledo where the Count of Belflor has just seduced Fénix, but he refuses to honor his promise to marry her because of the difference in their social rank. The count is forced to hide when Don Luis de Céspedes, father of Fénix, arrives. He is upset because he has received a letter from his son Pedro, a student at Salamanca who has gambled away all his money for registration, room and board. The letter is a model of youthful candor and cajolery: *"Jesus, Mary and Joseph.* —Father and Sir: By the present letter you will know that I have gambled away my money for the term; but you can take consolation in the fact that I lost it on the second-highest hand, and that will not happen to me again because I have taken an oath not to call a bet without having the cards in my hand. You know that one who has nothing to eat suffers the pain of death: you have the obligation to feed me because I didn't ask you to beget me . . . I'm sending Crispinillo to you there; you send him back right away with the *plus,* also known by the name *pecunia.* God keep you, my dear dad, old man of my heart, light of my eyes . . . Your humble son, *Perico."* [11] As already seen in the tragedies based on father-son conflicts, Rojas' sons are never hesitant about reminding their fathers that they engendered

[119]

them for their own pleasure, and, hence, are "indebted" to them. In this play that notion becomes the stuff of comedy.

Crispinillo's account of Pedro's roistering, carousing, and wenching at Salamanca does little to appease the old man's concern about his son's irresponsibility, but Don Luis decides to send him the money. After Crispinillo has departed, Don Luis goes to the balcony to call him back, and discovers the count who has just emerged from Fénix' room. Apprised of the truth but too old to avenge himself, he resolves to send for his son to restore the family's honor.

Meanwhile, Pedro has returned to Toledo where he is paying court to Casandra, sister of the Count of Belflor and of Arnesto. Informed of the affair, the latter has engaged professional assassins to kill Pedro, but in the melee, Arnesto is killed by Pedro, and the assassins are put to flight when the count, unaware of what has happened, arrives on the scene and gives Pedro refuge in his home. Advised by the police that Pedro killed his brother, the count permits him to leave but swears to seek him out to kill him.

In Act II, warned that a man whom he offended in Madrid has come to kill him, the count decides, nevertheless, to visit Fénix in her new home. Pedro, not knowing the identity of his sister's offender, comes to seek the count's help in restoring his family's honor, arguing that only when he has recovered his honor will he be an enemy worthy of him. The count agrees, permitting Pedro to protect him from his would-be assailant on his visit to Fénix. They proceed to the new house of Pedro's family (which he does not recognize) where Don Luis surprises his offender. Learning of the seduction of his sister, Pedro starts to attack the count, but the latter reminds him of his promise to protect him even at the cost of his own honor. In spite of his father's anger, Pedro permits his enemy to leave unharmed. Now obligated to one another but offended by each other ("obligados y ofendidos"), the two men resolve to avenge themselves.

In Act III, in order to protect Fénix from her family, the Count of Belfor takes her to his home where he entrusts her to the care of his sister Casandra. Meanwhile, arrested for killing Arnesto, Pedro becomes friendly with his fellow inmates, a gang of assassins from whom he learns that they have been hired by the offended Madrilenian to kill the count that very night. After the count frees Pedro from jail, they repeat their vows of friendship and enmity.

While going to comply with the challenge he received from the Madrilenian, the count is attacked by the thugs; but informed of the ambush, Pedro arrives to put them to flight. The two men then draw swords and begin to duel, but they both realize that their obligations to each other outweigh the offenses they have suffered. They agree that the count will marry Fénix and Pedro will marry Casandra.

In summary, Pedro and the Count of Belflor are bound in enmity by mutual honor offenses, Pedro having killed the count's brother and the count having seduced Pedro's sister, but so great do their obligations to each other become (among other things, each saves the other's life) that they are obliged to become friends. Although most Golden Age dramatists avoid bloodshed in their cape-and-sword plays, Rojas was especially concerned with finding peaceful solutions to honor offenses. That is not to say, however, that his characters are not sensitive to the demands of the honor code. One of the most interesting features of *Obligados y ofendidos* is that Pedro, despite his youthful extravagance and irresponsibility toward his university studies, reacts like a wounded bull when his honor is threatened.

Obligados y ofendidos enjoyed unusual popularity in France. It was translated or adapted by three French playwrights: Paul Scarron, *L'Écolier de Salamanque ou les Généreux Ennemis;* François Le Metel de Boisrobert, *Les Généreux Ennemis*; and Thomas Corneille, *Les Illustres Ennemis* (which also includes scenes from Calderón's *Amar después de la muerte* and *El pintor de su deshonra*). All three imitations of Rojas' play belong to 1654, a fact which Cotarelo called "truly singular." [12]

V *Primero es la honra que el gusto*

Not printed during Rojas' lifetime but preserved in several incomplete *sueltas,* mainly of the eighteenth century, *Primero es la honra que el gusto* has a badly mutilated third act of less than 500 verses. It is Rojas' most conventional cape-and-sword play and the least original. Its hackneyed plot is occasionally enlivened by a pair of sprightly servants, Pepino and Flora, but they do not compensate for the many trite situations. Perhaps it is significant that Rojas did not see fit to include it in the two *Partes* of his plays.

Both Don Félix and Don Juan are in love with Leonor, but although she loves Félix, her father Don Rodrigo insists that she marry Don Juan because, "If Don Juan is stupid, he is rich, Leonor, and in these times the one who is worth more can do more" (*BAE*, I, 441c). Ironically, Don Rodrigo, who knows nothing of his daughter's affection for his friend Félix, plans to seek his help in persuading Leonor to marry Don Juan. Félix, meanwhile, receives a letter from his former sweetheart Violante, who chides him for neglecting her, but before he can read it, it is intercepted by Flora, who turns it over to her mistress, Leonor. The latter comes to remonstrate with Félix, who has just given refuge to an unknown woman (Doña Ana) who is trying to escape from the importunities of Don Juan. Not only is Félix forced to hide Ana from Leonor but he must also conceal the latter from her father when he arrives. From this point on the intrigue becomes more complicated, as all the characters become involved in a series of bewildering incidents.

Finally, Leonor warns Don Juan that if he persists in marrying her against her will she will dishonor him, "Because a bold woman will trample on anybody's honor to gain revenge" (*BAE*, III, 451c). Then confronted by Doña Ana who threatens to avenge herself on him if he does not fulfill his obligations to her, Don Juan promises her that he will not marry Leonor. These words are overheard by Don Rodrigo, who insists that Don Juan marry his daughter the next day or suffer the consequences. Don Juan excuses himself on the grounds that Leonor threatened to dishonor him, and, as the title puts it, "Honor comes before pleasure." (Many lines are missing at this point.) Don Rodrigo threatens to kill Don Félix, but the latter explains that he has long been in love with Leonor and wishes to marry her if Don Rodrigo will accept him. The bewildered father accedes. Pepino announces that he will marry Flora.

In spite of its conventionality, *Primero es la honra que el gusto* bears Rojas' unmistakable stamp in the intensity of the conflict between Leonor and her father over the marriage into which he attempts to force her. Don Rodrigo's unabashed opportunism in wanting to marry his daughter to a wealthy man, no matter how boorish, is a common trait of many fathers in the Golden Age theater; and a daughter's determination to marry the man of her choice, at any cost, is not limited to Rojas' heroines. What is new here is Leonor's effrontery in telling Don Juan that she will dishonor him if he marries her. No self-respecting male, honor code or no code, would want to risk having such a wife.

VI *Sin honra no hay amistad*

Included in the *Segunda parte* of Rojas' plays (1645), *Sin honra no hay amistad* has been frequently mentioned as one of several plays that Agustín Moreto drew upon for the composition of his masterpiece, *El desdén con el desdén* (printed in 1654). The relationship between the two plays, studied by Mabel M. Harlan,[13] will be discussed briefly after a short summary of Rojas' play is given.

Melchor, a veteran of the wars in Flanders, and Antonio, a student at the University of Salamanca, have been close friends since childhood. They now share the same room and the same servant Sabañón, who, as a *gracioso estudiante,* is fond of making allusions to mythological characters and spouting Latin. Both friends have grievances: Melchor because his father was killed in a duel by an unidentified assailant, Antonio because his sister was abducted by an unknown man. To make matters worse, both friends are also in love, a fact which prevents them from giving full attention to avenging their honor. Before they can reveal the names of their sweethearts, they are interrupted when Melchor receives word that his lady has consented to see him and Sabañón reports to Antonio that he has learned the whereabouts of his sister.

It turns out that both friends are in love with Doña Juana, sister of Don Bernardo who abducted Antonio's sister, Inés, and seduced her under the promise of marriage. Inés now lives with Juana and Bernardo, and although her abductor has tired of her (he tells her, "If you loved me less, I would love you more"), Inés remains a staunch defender of men. Juana, on the other hand, is a militant feminist (like Laura in Lope de Vega's *La vengadora de las mujeres*) who has resolved to avenge her sex on all men because of their deceitfulness in dealing with women. Her strategy is to lead men on until she has conquered their hearts and then reject them. She falls into her own trap, however, when the astute Sabañón, on to her game, advises his masters to change their tactics and give her a dose of her own medicine. Accordingly, Melchor and Antonio pretend to pay court to her neighbor's daughters, whereupon Doña Juana, humiliated and tormented by jealousy, finds herself in love with both men.

Later, concealed in Bernardo's home, the two friends overhear him confesss that he killed Melchor's father and abducted Antonio's sister. They emerge, arguing over who should have priority in duelling with their offender, but their argument is cut short when Bernardo, whose honor has also been compromised by their presence in his sister's room, attacks them both. So great is their admiration for one another's skill and courage, however, that Antonio proposes a peaceful solution: that Bernardo make amends by marrying Inés and that Melchor marry Juana. All parties agree. Antonio, who is happy to remain a bachelor, is congratulated by Sabañón for his good fortune.

As indicated by the title, *Sin honra no hay amistad* is primarily, but not too seriously, concerned with examining the delicate balance between honor and friendship in the case of Melchor and Antonio, who are in love with the same woman, and with demonstrating that a peaceful solution to honor offenses can be reached when the aggrieved parties are basically honorable men of good will. As we have seen, the latter idea is also central to Rojas' *Obligados y ofendidos*. Only in a subordinate way does *Sin honra no hay amistad* treat the theme of combatting disdain with disdain.

There are, however, definite similarities between Rojas' play and Moreto's *El desdén con el desdén*. As Harlan has pointed out, there is considerable character equivalence since "Juana corresponds to Diana, Sabañón to Polilla, Melchor, generally speaking, to Carlos, and Inés, to a slight extent, to Cintia . . ." [14] The greatest similarity is in the roles of the two *graciosos,* for just as Polilla, the self-styled "doctor of love" (*médico de amor*), initiates and directs Carlos' campaign to bring Diana to her knees, so Sabañón, who calls himself a "surgeon" (*cirujano*), advises his masters to counter Juana's disdain with a show of disdain on their part.

Although Rojas' play is not as rich as Moreto's in psychological subtlety, its situations and characters are far from dull. One can understand Doña Juana's contempt for men in view of her brother's behavior toward Inés and in view of the letters she receives from ridiculous suitors who cannot wait to get in bed with her. Rojas was fond of using prose letters for humorous effects, especially to reveal the eccentricities of the writers. As in *Entre bobos anda el juego* in which Don Lucas reveals his crass materialism by carrying on all his correspondence concerning his marriage in commercial terms and by signing a receipt for the delivery of his bride, so in *Sin honra no hay amistad* Juana's suitors caricaturize themselves in their love letters to her. Here is part of a sample letter, one from a forthright youth who has a rich mother:

"My dear Juana: I don't know what the devil you have in that little face of yours that has made me want to make you love me. I well know that I can't match your beauty: What would I lack if I were as beautiful as you? . . . [But] let's stop the compliments and get to the point: my mother is very rich, and she is so old that she'll die within a year, give or take a month . . . I beg you to send me a binding marriage contract in which you obligate yourself to sleep with me when we are married. I promise it won't go badly for you. God keep you." [15]

It is no wonder that Juana finds men rather boorish.

CHAPTER 8

The Comedies of Manners

and Customs

OLDER historians of the Spanish stage usually took pains to distinguish between the *comedias de capa y espada* and the *comedias de costumbres,* a distinction which I regard as a valid one although at times it is hard to make. Writing more than a hundred years ago, George Ticknor sought to capture the essence of the cape-and-sword plays by saying that "their main and moving principle is gallantry," while the comedies of customs are "devoted to common life and the humbler classes."[1] Other differences between the two types are readily apparent.

As noted in the previous chapter, the cape-and-sword plays have rather stereotyped characters and a very complicated plot in which love, jealousy, and honor are invariably important motives. They focus less on ordinary happenings in daily life than on extraordinary events in the lives of a special breed of people who risk all in their constant pursuit of love. The fact that the action of these plays is often played out against a background of familiar landmarks of Spanish cities only lends them an illusion of reality. The *comedias de costumbres,* on the other hand, generally give little importance to plot. Their characters (although not necessarily of the "humbler classes" of which Ticknor spoke) represent a cross section of Spanish society—students, courtesans, lonesome widows, petty officials, businessmen—but they are not average people in that they all have peculiar quirks and a personal angle. Love, jealousy, and honor figure in these plays, but they are subordinated to the characters' abiding desire for comfort and security.

Of the four plays treated in this chapter, *Abre el ojo, Lo que son mujeres, Lo que quería ver el Marqués de Villena,* and

The Comedies of Manners and Customs

Entre bobos anda el juego, the last-named is a *comedia de costumbres* of a special kind. Since its principal character is a *figurón*, a ridiculous figure who is as different as can be from the usual heroes of romantic comedies, the play is the foremost representative of a type called the *comedia de figurón*. However, since Rojas' play not only includes several caricaturized characters but also involves amusing parodies of contemporary manners and customs, it is treated here with the *comedias de costumbres*.

The English writer Gerald Brenan has commented perceptively on some of Rojas' comedies of manners and customs in *The Literature of the Spanish People* (New York, 1957): "Where he broke new ground was in three of his lighter comedies—*Abre el ojo*, *Lo que son mujeres* and *Entre bobos anda el juego*. These are delightfully humorous plays, offering a rich variety of bores and pompous persons and thus throwing over the convention by which humor had to be confined to the *gracioso*. Like all comedies of cloak and sword, their plots consist in a juggling feat with endless embarrassing situations and misunderstandings, but the intrigue is not too closely woven (the fault of most of these Spanish comedies is the over-ingenuity of the plot) and allows for comic passages of great brilliance." (p. 312)

Brenan goes on to say that in these plays (which abound in those trifles of daily life which the Spaniards call *costumbrismo*) Rojas "enlarges the focus of literary consciousness by incorporating material that had never been used previously." "Yet we must be careful not to exaggerate the scope of his innovations. Rojas was a man of instinct rather than a self-conscious artist, and he failed to press on in the direction in which his intuitions were leading him." (*Ibid.*, pp. 312, 313)

I *Abre el ojo*

Published in the *Segunda parte* of 1645, *Abre el ojo* (printed elsewhere under the title of *Abrir el ojo*), together with *Lo que son mujeres*, represents Rojas' best effort to dramatize in a comical vein the manners and customs of one segment of Madrilenian society. The result is one of the most candid *costumbrista* plays to be found in the Spanish theater, and one which anticipates the *sainetes* of Ramón de la Cruz in the eighteenth century.

In *Abre el ojo* Rojas seems to make a deliberate effort to break away from most of the conventions of cape-and-sword drama to present a more realistic view of Madrilenian life. The usual romantic lovers are replaced by practical men and women whose chief concern is to satisfy their sexual and economic needs. There are no suspicious fathers or brothers to act as watchdogs over the women, and the women themselves certainly do not put a high premium on their honor. There is a duel which neither of the contestants takes very seriously, although one of them does denounce emphatically the provision of the duelling code that each party must be attended by a second, a provision which discomfits persons who had no part in the quarrel. The point is that everybody in the play is looking out for his own comfort, and he fully expects everyone else to do the same. One other feature which enhances the *costumbrismo* of *Abre el ojo* is the frequent reference to the streets, squares, and public places of Madrid. Rojas loved his adopted city, but the reader needs a guidebook to follow his characters' meanderings through it.

The plot revolves around the efforts of Don Clemente to keep his women friends from meeting each other, and the efforts of Doña Clara to keep her men friends apart. Neither is successful, although each invents a number of ruses for the purpose. Don Clemente is beset by a persistent widow, Doña Hipólita, with whom he has been having an affair for six years, but although she provides him an orderly, domestic life, he has begun to tire of her. In the opening scene of the play, he does not hesitate to tell her that he is bored with her, a scene, as Carlos Ortigoza has observed, that is remarkable for its frankness and bold modernity.[2]

Don Clemente is attracted to Doña Clara, as she is to him, but she is too concerned about her comfort to let love stand in the way. A *dama del tusón* (a type of courtesan about whom Lope de Vega wrote so knowingly), Clara manages for a while to keep four men friends on the string, although she has to change apartments to keep them from becoming aware of each other's existence. She even inveigles two of her lovers into buying furniture for her new apartment, each paying a different sum according to his means and generosity. In the final scene of the play, when Clemente's women friends and Clara's men friends learn the facts, they are brought together in two choruses to give warning ("abre el ojo") of the deceits of the opposite sex. Because of its candid portrait of the relationships between the sexes, its piquant language, and its realism, *Abre el ojo* stands as one of the most modern Golden Age comedies of manners.

II *Lo que son mujeres*

Published in the *Segunda parte* of 1645, *Lo que son mujeres* is a light comedy and an unusual one for its time. It has little plot, it has few situations that are truly dramatic, it does not involve honor, and it does not even have a *gracioso*. It does, however, contain a number of grotesque characters whose freakish personalities and strange antics provide the fun. Valbuena Prat, in trying to find a suitable classification for the play, called it an "amplification of the *entremés.*"

The plot, such as it is, centers upon the different attitudes of two sisters toward men. As her father's heiress, Serafina is not only rich but beautiful, cold, and disdainful. Matea, on the other hand, is homely and not very bright, but she loves men— all men. For this reason, Serafina continually threatens to send her to a convent. Hearing of Serafina's beauty and fortune, Gibaja, a professional matchmaker, comes to see her hoping to arrange her marriage at a nice profit for himself. Completely frank about the tricks of his trade, Gibaja persuades Serafina to see four suitors that he has lined up for her. They are as odd as Gibaja made them out to be: one is a constant grumbler (a Spanish Heraclitus, Serafina calls him); the second is a complacent bore (a Democritus); the third, a Latin-spouting pedant; the fourth, a banal fool who can speak only in clichés. They resemble nothing as much as escapees from a Ben Jonson "humours" play. Serafina, of course, openly disdains the whole lot of them, but Matea finds them all to her liking.

Coached by Gibaja, the four suitors later pretend to disdain Serafina and to be in love with Matea, whose hand in marriage they request in writing. Of course, Serafina is miffed, and Matea is elated. Later, on the occasion of Matea's birthday, Serafina arranges a literary academy for which Gibaja writes a play. Not only is its title *Lo que son mujeres* but its main characters are identical to those of Rojas' comedy, that is, the four eccentric suitors and the two sisters. In short, the play-within-the-play is a mirror of *the* play. As in the literary academies of the period, whose activities Serafina's academy is meant to spoof, each suitor selects a theme on which he composes a poem indicative of his personal quirks. In conclusion, Matea, now sought after, becomes disdainful of all men; Serafina, now spurned, is willing to settle for any man but is rejected by all. Just as Cervantes ended his play *La entretenida* pointing out that it does not contain a marriage, so Rojas asks for the audience's applause, "because he wrote this play without a marriage or a death" (*BAE*, III, 211c).

Lo que son mujeres bears on the theme of overcoming disdain with disdain, but its chief interest resides in its characters (who are certainly not complex) and in its technique. It is one of the few Spanish plays of the Golden Age, if not the only one, which contains an inserted play that parallels the framing play on every count.

III *Lo que quería ver el Marqués de Villena*

Printed in the *Segunda parte* of 1645, this is a play about which little need be said. It has a slight plot and few dramatic situations; yet it is not vapid. It has a number of colorful scenes and several elements typical of Rojas' dramaturgy—a strong dose of feminism, a bathing nude, etc.—but these things do not add up to much.

The play begins with a flurry of action as the Castilian students at the University of Salamanca demonstrate noisily in favor of their candidate, Dr. Pedro Bermúdez, who is competing in the *oposiciones* for a professorial chair at the university. His chief rival for the professorship is Dr. Alonso de Madrid (called *el capón* because of a completely hairless face), who is backed by the Manchegan students. Although the supporters of the two candidates clash in the streets of Salamanca, Bermúdez, who feels strongly attracted to his rival, confides that he hopes Madrid wins the chair. Thanks to the art of the magician Fileno, who possesses a mirror capable of reflecting what is going on anywhere, it is revealed that Dr. Alonso de Madrid is in fact a woman, Doña Juana de Madrid, who came to Salamanca disguised as a man to prove that women are not intellectually inferior to men. She is also the woman to whom Pedro Bermúdez lost his heart when he saw her bathing in the nude, but whom he has not seen since.

Aside from a few more scenes having to do with student life at Salamanca (pranks committed against local shopkeepers, the reactions of students when their fathers fail to send them all the money they asked for, the frantic efforts to conceal a woman in a dormitory room when the proctor arrives), the rest of the play concerns an amorous quadrangle. Pedro Bermúdez loves Doña Juana but she loves the Marqués de Villena; the marqués, however, is in love with Serafina, but she is enamored of Doña Juana, who she does not know is a woman. And what is it that the Marqués de Villena wanted to see, a question raised several times during the play? The answer is: he wanted to see precisely the entangled loves represented in the plot, in which A loves B, B loves C, etc. The theme of the play, lightly treated as it is, is simply that those who love are doomed to frustration.

Cotarelo objects to the fact that a notable anachronism mars the play: the famous Enrique de Villena, called the Marqués de Villena, never attended the University of Salamanca and, moreover, he lived in the fifteenth century, fully two centuries before the action of Rojas' play presumably takes place. Oh well, any necromancer of the caliber of Villena should be able to be at a place where he never was two centuries after he ceased to be.

IV *Entre bobos anda el juego*

Rojas' fondness for burlesque, readily apparent in the comic subplots of his tragedies and in the main plots of plays like *Donde hay agravios no hay celos,* achieved culmination in *Entre bobos anda el juego* (probably written in 1638 but not printed until the *Segunda parte* of 1645). Rojas' play is often called the first *comedia de figurón* although it was preceded by Alonso de

Castillo Solórzano's *El Marqués de Cigarral* (1634) to which it owes, among other things, the surname of its principal character, Don Lucas de Cigarral. The *comedia de figurón* is usually defined as a play featuring a protagonist who is a supreme odd-ball: he is vain, arrogant, presumptuous, crass, loutish, and often freakish in appearance.[3] He is not just an exaggerated eccentric; he is often a ridiculous monomaniac. He is, in brief, anti-*galán*—the very opposite of the handsome, romantic, gallant heroes who abound in the cape-and-sword plays. Strangely, however, the *comedia de figurón* has been singled out as an effective vehicle for social criticism, since its burlesque tone affords the dramatist the freedom to satirize Spanish customs and institutions in a way which would be denied him in more serious plays.

Don Lucas de Cigarral is a wealthy squire from the environs of Toledo. He is a monomaniac and his mania is money, but he certainly does not believe in throwing it around. In fact, so tight is he, says a servant in making a verbal portrait of him, that he eats so little that he has no excrements. This, we are told, is his single grace. Engaged to the lovely Isabel whose betrothal was arranged against her will by her mercenary father—for this reason, some critics have held that the play involves a protest against parental choice of marital partners, in the same way as Moratín's *El sí de las niñas* does more than 150 years later—Don Lucas writes his first love letter to his fiancée. It begins, "Sister: I have 6042 ducats in income from my inheritance," and ends, "May God keep you and give you more children than me." He then sends Isabel's father a receipt for the bride-to-be.

Although Don Lucas is long on money matters, he is short on the small talk of romance. Accordingly, he makes the mistake of asking his cousin Don Pedro, who is secretly in love with Isabel, to express the sentiments and endearments expected of him. Pedro and Isabel debate in Don Lucas' presence whether true love can exist without the frequent and prolonged association (*trato*) of two persons. Rojas, who was fond of using repetition as a comic device, gives them this dialogue:

ISABEL:
    . . . for pleasure, it is essential to have association, since association is what engenders love.

PEDRO:
> I confess that love, with association, is perfect; but it should be understood that there can be love without association.

ISABEL:
> But, in short, love is increased by association.

PEDRO:
> That's right . . .

LUCAS:
> (I don't like these associations.) (*Aside.*)
> (Ed. F. Ruiz Morcuende, Act I, vv. 866–77)

As in many Spanish plays of the day, much of the action of *Entre bobos anda el juego* takes place on the road and in the inns en route from Madrid to Toledo, the swift action of the play being geared to the movement involved in the journey. It is at a wayside inn that Don Lucas learns that his fiancée and his cousin are carrying on their "association" behind his back. Although the figurón is said to be anti-*galán,* this does not mean that he has no sense of honor or that he is not incited to action when offended. To the contrary: when Don Lucas realizes that his honor has been outraged, he swears to take revenge on the lovers that will endure the rest of their lives, since to kill them would be, in his words, only "venial vengeance" and exactly what they want. Insisting that they marry, he then cuts them off without a cent so that they will face a lifetime of penury, with no other sustenance than their words of love: "and soon they'll learn what love is without stew" (vv. 2757-58).

Although Don Lucas dominates the play because of his queer antics, he is by no means the only strange character in it. His sister Alfonsa, who can swoon at will to achieve her ends, is not far behind him; and Don Luis, another of Isabel's unwelcome suitors who continually dogs her, is a perfect caricature of the extreme *cultiparlista.* Rojas, who is often criticized for his own Gongoristic poetry, never tired of satirizing the affected speech of ridiculous euphuists.

In addition to its bizarre characters, its comical situations, and its gay burlesque, what makes *Entre bobos* an especially delightful play is Rojas' control of language. Since one of the major concerns of the play is to ridicule those who reduce all human values to terms of dollars and cents, Rojas sought to communicate that concern by means of style. Although the conventions of the Spanish theater demanded that plays be written in verse, Rojas realized that the language of business is prose. Accordingly, Don Lucas' letter to Isabel (which is a business letter in the strictest sense) and the receipt that he gives her father when she is delivered to him are written in prose. And when Don Lucas is forced to speak to his bride-to-be in verse, his speech is little more than rhymed prose since marriage for him is simply another business deal.

On the other hand, Don Pedro, whose love for Isabel is "poetic," soars in rhapsodic flights when he talks about her. He fell in love with her when he first spied her bathing in the Manzanares River (just as David was smitten by the fair form of Bathsheba, so Rojas' heroes often lose their hearts to bathing nudes),[4] and his senses become inflamed as he describes her bath in 230 verses of verbal striptease. In short, the play involves two masterfully controlled levels of language, one for Don Lucas and his materialistic world, another for Don Pedro and his realm of pure passion.

Although *Entre bobos anda el juego* criticizes mercenary parents who seek to marry off their daughters for personal profit, although it satirizes the banal values of the upstart middle class, it is primarily a parody of romantic comedies in which love invariably triumphs. Don Lucas may be an eccentric dolt but his revenge, typical of his peculiar sense of values but unknown in the canons of the honor code, is an effective rejoinder to the conventional happy endings of cape-and-sword plays which forget to tell us if full hearts can survive empty stomachs.

CHAPTER 9

Conclusion

WHEN Rojas began writing for the stage about 1630, the Spanish theater had already undergone a long process of enrichment and refinement at the hands of Lope de Vega and his contemporaries. They had declared the independence of the national theater from the classical precepts, and, despite the demurrers of academic critics, they had succeeded in making the drama a popular art form. Together they had written thousands of plays based on a wide range of subjects. Although they seemingly had exhausted every source of plot, every dramatic situation, every theatrical device and trick, their creativity never ran dry. Lope himself, who dominated the Spanish theater for almost half a century, wrote one of his best plays, *El castigo sin venganza*, when he was in his seventieth year.

The generation of playwrights that followed Lope and his disciples was confronted with an enormous task: they could not compete with their predecessors in productivity, they could only try to improve upon their products. Calderón, leader of the new generation, set the pattern by perfecting the structure and dramatic unity of the *comedia*, enriching the characters, embellishing the style, and deepening the thematic content. How well he succeeded in improving upon the formal and substantial aspects of Spanish drama may be seen by comparing the recasts he made with the earlier plays which served him as sources.[1]

Rojas, like Calderón, was essentially a court dramatist whose plays were written primarily for an aristocratic audience. This fact determined in large measure not only their choice of material but also their treatment of it. Both dramatists reached maturity after the avant-garde poetry of Luis de Góngora became fashionable among literary sophisticates; both were deeply influenced by his brilliant innovations in poetic language.

But Rojas was a much less conscious artist than Calderón, less intellectual and less philosophical. He also lacked his friend's judgment and balance. Although he too improved upon the structure of the earlier *comedia*, he did so more because of his strong dramatic instinct than by reflection. At its best his instinct led him to the creation of tragic situations of an emotional intensity rarely equalled in the Golden Age. It also led him to the creation of comical scenes that would do credit to the greatest comic writers.

But Rojas was not only moved by instinct, for he deliberately sought to increase the popular appeal of his plays through the cultivation of sensationalism and by striving for effect. His alleged originality and boldness result, more often than not, from a conscious effort to be different. It is true, as Cotarelo remarked, that in the field of serious drama, "His daring led him to devise ultratragic situations (fratricides, filicides, rapes) and to present uncommon conflicts of honor,"[2] but one has the feeling that Rojas dramatized these things not so much to present a broader view of reality but to jolt his audience into attention. It is also true, as remarked by Valbuena Prat, that in the realm of comedy Rojas "was the most intense writer of comedy in the cycle of Calderón."[3] Fortunately, the distortion of reality for comic effect is more artful because comedy, unlike tragedy, does not ask us to believe.

In my monograph on Rojas' tragedies, I drew certain conclusions concerning his contributions to Spanish tragedy, conclusions which it may be well to summarize here. Most of the issues with which Rojas' tragedies deal (honor, revenge, father-son conflicts, heedless love) are not new with him. It is the way he treats them and resolves them—or leaves them unresolved—that is new. Unlike most of his contemporaries, Rojas viewed these issues, not so much in social or religious terms, but as they brought suffering to individual lives. He saw them, not as obstacles to be overcome to attain social or spiritual vindication, but as insoluble impediments to human happiness. There is in Rojas' tragedies—with rare exceptions—no solution through submission to higher authority than oneself. There is no escape.

Along with his insistence upon the inescapability of the tragic issue, there is in his tragedies a different focus upon the tragic protagonist. Rojas' characters, for the most part, follow only the impulses of their own hearts; but regardless of whether those impulses are noble or base, they lead inevitably to their undoing. They stake their lives on their ambitions, knowing full well (or they should know) that they cannot win. The greatest victory, says Segismundo in *La vida es sueño,* is victory over one's self. That cannot be, Rojas seems to say; people being what they are, reason can never dominate the passions. That is their tragedy.

Above all, Rojas' heroines, both in the tragedies and in the honor dramas, are noteworthy in Golden Age drama. They refuse to accept the notion that their grievances can serve only to spur men to action. When they are wronged, Lucrecia, Progne and Filomena, Medea, Rosimunda, and Isabel in *Cada cual lo que le toca* are incited to action to redress the offense, not to right things in a man's world but in their own. What happens to these women and the action they take are not just subsidiary issues; they form the crux of the plays. There is no need to wait until the eighteenth century to look for tragic heroines in the Spanish theater, as one critic has maintained.[4] They abound in Rojas' tragedies and honor dramas.

To a large degree Rojas' tragic art represents a return to Spanish tragedy as it was cultivated a half-century earlier by neo-Senecan dramatists—before Lope de Vega forged the new *comedia*. There are in Rojas' tragedies, as in those of Juan de la Cueva and his followers, the same concern with the Senecan themes of revenge and fortune, the same preoccupation with exaggerated tragic types, the same cult of violence, the same unrestrained expression of emotion. Most of these Senecan themes and practices persisted in the theater of Lope de Vega and his disciples where they were modified and refined but seldom left to stand alone as tragedy. They too became a part of the diverse ingredients that formed the new *comedia*. Heir to both the Cuevan and Lopean schools, Rojas seized upon the Senecanism of Cueva but fashioned his tragedies with the technical refinements and dramaturgical sophistication of Lope and Calderón.

Rojas' abiding desire to be different led to less happy results in his religious and novelistic plays than in the tragedies and honor dramas. Perhaps it would not be too condescending to say that he should be forgiven if his religious plays too often lack genuine religious feeling, that his *autos sacramentales* are not sacramental enough, and that his novelistic plays are rife with vacuous novelties. Ironically, most of these plays will be remembered, not for the purpose for which they were written, but because they underscore so heavily persistent traits of Rojas' dramaturgy. *Los trabajos de Tobías,* his only religious play which succeeds in uniting pathos and piety convincingly, sticks in the mind because of the savage grotesqueness of the scene of the blinding of Tobías. *La vida en el ataúd* is notable, not because of the saintliness of its protagonist, but because of the voluptuousness of its women and the sensuality of its love scenes. And *Los bandos de Verona* will be remembered only because of the firmness with which Rojas' Juliet opposes her father's desire to pick a husband for her. When all else fails in Rojas' plays, they can usually be counted on for some extremely grotesque scenes, voluptuous women, erotic love scenes, and girls who reject parental interference in affairs of the heart.

Critics will continue to debate over Rojas' merits as a tragedian and to find many faults with his religious and novelistic plays, but none has shown any inclination to dispute his talents as a comic writer. Indeed, one of the chief faults that some critics find with his serious plays is his penchant to disturb their mood with lengthy, and often bizarre, comical intrusions. There is no question that his strong comic verve and fondness for burlesque often led him to sacrifice integrity for laughter—as they also led him to create some of the most hilarious scenes in Spanish drama.

As examples of Rojas' "bad taste," one can point to Juanete's diarrhea and stomach cramps in *Progne y Filomena,* at the very moment when King Tereo is tracking down Filomena to rape her; or Buscaruidos' vain attempts in *El desafío de Carlos V* to elude the amorous hermaphrodite who continually pursues him; or the fear-crazed servants in *La vida en el ataúd* and *El mejor amigo el muerto* (saints' plays, both) who run around the stage trying to protect their buttocks against their enema-minded enemies who advance upon them armed with syringes; or the bickering peasant couple, Tronco and Olalla, in the

[138]

Conclusion

Numantia plays who continue to abuse each other to the very last, as their fellow townsmen starve to death about them. One also remembers Rojas' "good" comic scenes (which may be no less grotesque than the "bad" ones) and the acute verbal skill with which they are written: Cabellera's description of Don Lucas de Cigarral in *Entre bobos anda el juego;* Testuz staggering about the stage in *El profeta falso Mahoma* eulogizing the seven *hermanitos* of Spanish wines which he has "killed off" in a burlesque of the ballad of *Las cabezas de los siete infantes de Lara;* the mock tragedy in *Cada cual lo que le toca* in which Beltrán, dagger in hand, witnesses the seduction of his wife but, like his master in the main plot, is too irresolute or too cowardly to act. Rarely in Spanish drama has a comic subplot been used so effectively to invest the main plot with irony.

Rojas' chief contributions to Spanish comedy, it seems to me, lie in two different areas. On one hand, without changing or adding substantially to the characteristics of the *gracioso* himself (as those characteristics had been established by Lope de Vega and his contemporaries), he gave the *gracioso* a more prominent role by fabricating elaborate comic subplots in which that stock character necessarily became the leading character, or by making him a central character (not a supporting one) in the main intrigue of the plot. On the other hand, Rojas invented a series of plays, the comedies of manners and customs, in which the humor does not depend on the *gracioso* (indeed, some of them do not have a *gracioso* at all) but on a variety of characters whose foibles and eccentricities lead to comical situations and incongruities of great diversity.

As examples of the first tendency, one can cite *No hay amigo para amigo* and *Donde hay agravios no hay celos,* both cape-and-sword plays. In the former, the comic subplot does not dominate the play (as it does in Paul Scarron's adaptation, *Le Jodolet duelliste*), but the enmity between Moscón and Fernando, leading to their proposed duel, involves them in prominent roles independent of the main plot. Although Moscón's cowardice (a conventional trait of Lope's *graciosos*) prevents him from going through with the duel, the very length of the subplot gives him (or Rojas) an opportunity to scoff at the honor code more thoroughly than former *graciosos* whose cowardice also prompts them to repudiate the demands of honor. In *Donde hay agravios,* in which the whole plot hinges on the exchange of roles of master and servant, the *gracioso* necessarily becomes a principal character in the action. Although other dramatists of Rojas' generation gave prominence to the *gracioso,* especially Agustín Moreto whose Polilla in *El desdén con el desdén* is indispensable to the plot, in no Spanish play of the period other than *Donde hay agravios* does the *gracioso* become, so to speak, the leading man. The possibilities for humor produced by the exchange of roles were many, of course, and Rojas did not fail to exploit them as Sancho swaggers about outraging polite society with his boorish conduct. One thing should be noted about both *No hay amigo para amigo* and *Donde hay agravios,* however, and that is that the humor is really at the expense of the *gracioso,* not at the expense of the audience. Burlesque, unlike satire, does not force people to laugh at themselves.

The humor of the comedies of manners and customs is deeper and more complex simply because it springs from an exposé of plausible human weaknesses and vanities, not from ridiculing a professional funny man. *Entre bobos anda el juego* presents a special case, of course, since the *figurón* is more skillfully caricaturized than any *gracioso* who ever walked a Spanish stage. For the most part, however, the people who fill these plays are credible human beings, and it is to Rojas' credit that he perceived that humor could be gained by treating them sympathetically, not just by lampooning them. These plays suggest that Rojas was forming a new concept of comedy, but unfortunately, as Brenan observed, "he failed to press on in the direction in which his intuitions were leading him." [5]

We must, of course, judge Rojas by what he wrote, not by what he might have written had circumstances been different. One can only conjecture whether he would have continued to develop a broader and more modern conception of theatrical art if his career had not been cut short by the closing of the Spanish theaters in 1644 and his premature death in 1648.

Notes and References

List of Abbreviations

BN   Biblioteca Nacional (National Library, Madrid)

BAE   *Biblioteca de Autores Españoles (Library of Spanish Authors)*. Unless otherwise stated, the abbreviation refers to Vol. LIV, *Comedias escogidas de don Francisco de Rojas,* ordenadas en colección por don Ramón de Mesonero Romanos (*Selected Plays of Francisco de Rojas,* arranged in a Collection by Ramón de Mesonero Romanos), Madrid, 1866. The Roman numerals I, II, and III are used to indicate the act numbers.

Parte I *Primera parte de las comedias de Don Francisco de Rojas Zorrilla (Volume I of the Plays of Francisco de Rojas Zorrilla),* Madrid, 1640.

Parte II *Segunda parte de las comedias de Don Francisco de Rojas Zorrilla (Volume II of the Plays of Francisco de Rojas Zorrilla),* Madrid, 1645.

Chapter One

1. At Cotarelo's request, Unamuno searched the matriculation lists of the University of Salamanca for the period when Rojas was likely in attendance, but he found no trace of the dramatist's name. This does not rule out the possibility of Rojas' attendance there but leaves it in doubt.

2. *Para todos, exemplos morales, humanos, y divinos . . .* (Sevilla: Imprenta de los Gómez, 1736), p. 511.

3. H. A. Rennert, *The Spanish Stage in the Time of Lope de Vega* (New York: The Hispanic Society of America, 1909), p. 519.

4. Emilio Cotarelo y Mori, *Don Francisco de Rojas Zorrilla, noticias biográficas y bibliográficas* (Madrid: Imprenta de la *Revista de Archivos,* 1911), p. 39.

5. *Ibid.,* pp. 40-41.

6. H. C. Lancaster, *A History of French Dramatic Literature in the Seventeenth Century* (Baltimore: The Johns Hopkins University Press, 1929), Part II, Vol. II, pp. 458-59, states that Scarron's adaptation of Rojas' play, *Jodolet ou le maître valet* (1645), enjoyed considerable success on the French stage. It was performed fifteen times by Molière's troupe between 1659 and 1662 and 217 times at the Comédie Française between 1680 and 1791.

7. Cotarelo, *op. cit.*, pp. 43-53, gives an extensive account of these festivities.

8. Rojas' *vejamen* of 1637 is printed in Antonio Paz y Melia, *Sales españolas*, segunda serie (Madrid: Imprenta de la *Revista de Archivos*, 1902), pp. 311-22, and also in Antonio Pérez Gómez' edition of *Academia burlesca en Buen Retiro a la Magestad de Philippo IV el Grande* (Valencia: Tip. Moderna, 1952), pp. 124-32.

9. The *vejamen* of 1638, edited by Manuel Serrano y Sanz, is printed as an appendix in A. Bonilla's edition of Luis Vélez de Guevara, *El diablo cojuelo* (Vigo: Librería de Eugenio Krapf, 1902), pp. 262-71.

10. The anonymous *Avisos* are contained in a manuscript located in the Biblioteca Nacional in Madrid, No. 2339.

11. H. W. Hilborn, *A Chronology of the Plays of D. Pedro Calderón de la Barca* (Toronto: The University of Toronto Press, 1938), p. 114. As a matter of fact, Rojas probably wrote fewer *autos* during this period than Calderón. The authorship of six *autos* attributed to him by Cotarelo may be questioned.

12. Francisco Arquero Soria, *La Virgen de Atocha*, Temas Madrileños, Vol. VIII (Madrid: Instituto de Estudios Madrileños, 1954), pp. 35-36.

13. Casiano Pellicer, *Tratado histórico sobre el origen y progresos de la comedia y del histrionismo en España* (Madrid: Imprenta de la Administración del Real Arbitrio de Beneficencia, 1804), II, 57, refrains from mentioning Rojas by name as the father of Francisca Bezón, saying only: "She was the daughter of one of the best known and most noble writers who supplied the theaters in the time of Philip IV with plays . . ." Cotarelo has demonstrated that Juan Bezón was the stage name of Rojas' illegitimate half-brother, Gregorio de Rojas. He gives the year of Francisca Bezón's death as 1703 instead of 1704 (p. 304).

14. In the *Bulletin of the Comediantes*, IX (1957), 7-9, I adduced certain evidence (but not proof) to indicate that Rojas alone did not write *Del rey abajo, ninguno*, although I suggested the possibility that he collaborated in its composition. I have discovered no evidence to indicate that the play written by Rojas, Calderón, and Solís was in fact *Del rey abajo*.

15. Rennert, *op. cit.*, p. 246.

16. Cotarelo, *op. cit.*, pp. 14-15.

17. Gregorio Marañón, *El Conde-Duque de Olivares* (Madrid: Espasa-Calpe, 1936), pp. 177, 325. The same Francisco de Chiriboga (or Chiriboya) was a witness at Rojas' wedding.

18. Cotarelo, *op. cit.*, p. 83, does not hesitate to identify this Francisco de Quevedo as the great satirical writer who returned to the court from house arrest in San Marcos after the fall of Olivares in 1643. I am not so sure, since another man by the same name served during the same period as secretary for affairs of the military orders.

19. *Autos sacramentales, con cuatro comedias nuevas, y sus loas, y entremeses. Primera parte* (Madrid: María de Quiñones, 1655), p. 45.

20. *Ibid.*, p. 47.

21. *Ibid.*, p. 56.

Chapter Two

1. See Cotarelo, *op. cit.*, pp. 273-78. The enemy of the theater was Fray Francisco de Rojas, a Franciscan monk, who wrote a diatribe against the drama under the misleading title of *Apologías trágicas. Primera, y segunda parte* (n.p., 1654). He is especially vitriolic in condemning his fellow ecclesiastics for attending plays.

2. "Apuntes biográficos, bibliográficos y críticos . . . de Rojas," in Mesonero's edition of the *Comedias escogidas de don Francisco de Rojas Zorrilla*, Vol. LIV of the *Biblioteca de Autores Españoles* (Madrid: M. Rivadeneyra, 1866), p. x.

3. In the prologue to his edition of Rojas' *Teatro*, vol. 35 of *Clásicos Castellanos* (Madrid: Espasa-Calpe, 1944), pp. xxiii-xxvi.

4. Rojas concluded the prologue of his *Segunda parte* with the statement that if it was well received, he would publish a third part, but it was never printed.

5. Rennert, *The Spanish Stage*, p. 122.

6. Brief but good definitions of metrical forms are found in S. G. Morley and C. Bruerton, *The Chronology of Lope de Vega's "comedias"* (New York, The Modern Language Association of America, 1940), pp. 11-13. Dorothy L. Duis, "Versification in the *comedias* of Rojas Zorrilla" (unpublished Master's thesis, Ohio State University, 1926), has studied the versification of thirty-eight plays attributed to Rojas, several of which are apocryphal.

7. See note 14 to Chapter 1.

8. See Américo Castro, "Obras mal atribuídas a Rojas Zorrilla," *Revista de Filología Española*, III (1916), 66-68.

9. *History of Spanish Literature*, 4th ed. (Boston: James R. Osgood, 1872), II, p. 440.

10. Ludwig Pfandl, *Historia de la literatura nacional española en la edad de oro*, translated from the German by J. R. Balaguer, 2nd ed. (Barcelona: Editorial Gustavo Gili, 1952), p. 466.

Chapter Three

1. In H. J. Chaytor, ed. *Dramatic Theory in Spain* (Cambridge: The University Press, 1925), vv. 174 ff.

2. Quoted by Eduardo Juliá Martínez, ed. *Poetas dramáticos valencianos* (Madrid: Imp. de la *Revista de Archivos, Bibliotecas y Museos*, 1929), I, 623. The translation is mine, as are all future ones unless otherwise stated.

3. *Ibid.*

4. For a general treatment of critical response to the Lopean *comedia*, see Joaquín de Entrambasaguas, "Una guerra literaria del Siglo de Oro: Lope de Vega y los preceptistas aristotélicos," *Boletín de la Real Academia Española*, XIX (1932), 135-60, 260-326; XX (1933), 405-44, 569-600, 687-734; XXI (1934), 82-112, 238-72, 423-62, 587-628, 795-857.

5. Cf. Edwin S. Morby, "Some observations on 'tragedia' and 'tragicomedia' in Lope," *Hispanic Review*, XI (1943), 185-209.

6. Ed. C. F. Adolfo Van Dam (Groninga: P. Nordhoff, 1928), pp. 10-11.

7. F. S. Escribano, "Cuatro contribuciones españolas a la preceptiva dramática mundial," *Bulletin of the Comediantes*, XIII (Spring, 1961), p. 3, n. 4.

8. Alberto Lista, *Ensayos literarios y críticos*, two vols. in one (Seville: Calvo-Rubio, 1844), II, 86, 136-37; George Ticknor, *History of Spanish Literature*, 4th ed. (New York: James R. Osgood, 1872), II, 492; Eugenio de Ochoa, *Tesoro del teatro español* (Paris: Baudry, 1838), IV, 338; A. F. von Schack, *Historia de la literatura y el arte dramático en España*, trans. E. de Mier (Madrid: Imprenta y Fundición de M. Tello, 1885-1887), V, 47-49; Cayetano Alberto de la Barrera y Leirado, *Catálogo bibliográfico y biográfico del teatro antiguo español* . . . (Madrid: M. Rivadeneyra, 1860), p. 340: "Respecto al carácter de sus composiciones dramáticas, Rojas, más inclinado al género trágico, se aventajó en él a todos sus contemporáneos."

9. Ramón de Mesonero Romanos, "Apuntes biográficos, bibliográficos y críticos," in his edition of Rojas' plays, Vol. 54 of the *Biblioteca de Autores Españoles* (Madrid: M. Rivadeneyra, 1866), p. xx.

10. M. Menéndez y Pelayo, *Estudios y discursos de crítica histórica y literaria*, ed. Enrique Sánchez Reyes (Santander: Consejo Superior de Investigaciones Científicas, 1941), III, 291; E. Cotarelo y Mori, *Don Francisco de Rojas Zorrilla* . . . (Madrid: Imp. de la *Revista de Archivos*, 1911), p. 119; A. Valbuena Prat, *Literatura dramática española* (Barcelona: Editorial Labor, 1930), pp. 249-50; F. C. Sáinz de Robles, *El teatro español, historia y antología* (Madrid: Aguilar, 1943), III, 37-39.

Notes and References

11. Juan Hurtado y Angel González Palencia, *Historia de la literatura española*, 4th ed. (Madrid: SAETA, 1943), pp. 688, 690. Cf. Pfandl, *op. cit.*, p. 466.

12. Caimán's description of the meeting of Marco Antonio and Cleopatra at the Cydnus River (205 verses of *romance, BAE*, II, 429c-30a) is very similar to Enobarbus' account of their meeting in Shakespeare's play. Both accounts derive from Plutarch.

13. *BAE*, I, 424a: "Y mis ojos navegaron/ Las ondas de su cabello:/ Aneguéme en su hermosura . . ."

14.   *La Venus de Alejandría*
    Y el romano más dichoso,
    Bebiéndose están amantes
    Las dos almas por los ojos.
    De Octaviano, que es su amigo,
    Faltó a la fe y al decoro,
    Que en estando el amor ciego,
    No ve al amistad tampoco.
             (*BAE*, II, 433b.)

15. For a history of the play, see the introduction to my edition (Albuquerque: The University of New Mexico Press, 1963). All citations to the text are to this edition.

16. However, Joseph E. Gillet, "Lucrecia—necia," *Hispanic Review*, XV (1947), 120-36, has demonstrated that several sixteenth and seventeenth-century Spanish writers, following the lead of St. Augustine, took an unsympathetic, and even cynical, attitude toward Lucretia and her self-destruction.

17. Benedetto Croce, *Storia dell Età barocca in Italia* (Bari: Laterza y Figli, 1957), p. 445.

18. Cf. Seneca, *Of a Happy Life*: "He that can look death in the face, and bid it welcome . . . this is the man whom Providence has established in the possession of inviolable rights." "We must, therefore, escape from them [pleasure and pain] into freedom. This nothing will bestow upon us save contempt of Fortune . . ." In Kevin Guinagh and Alfred Dorjahn, eds. *Latin Literature in Translation* (New York: Longmans, Green and Co., 1950), pp. 597, 599.

19. *Romvlvs and Tarquin, Written in Italian by the Marques Virgilio Malvezzi. And now taught English by Henry Earle of Monmouth,* 3rd ed. (*London*, 1648), p. 186.

20. Aristotle, *On the Art of Poetry*, trans. S. H. Butcher (New York: The Liberal Arts Press, 1948), p. 16.

21. Raymond R. MacCurdy, *Francisco de Rojas Zorrilla and the Tragedy* (Albuquerque: The University of New Mexico Press, 1958), pp. 72-73.

22. Cf. Mesonero Romanos, *op. cit.*, p. xx.

23. Cf. Fredson T. Bowers, *Elizabethan Revenge Tragedy, 1587-1642* (Princeton: Princeton University Press, 1940), *passim*. A critical study of Rojas' play is found in my edition of the play, Vol. 153 of *Clásicos Castellanos* (Madrid, 1961), pp. xxviii-xl. All citations are to this edition.

24. The sources of the play are studied by Joaquín de Entrambasaguas in "La leyenda de Rosamunda," *Revista Bibliográfica y Documental*, II (1948), 339-89.

25. The ballad is included in Agustín Durán, *Romancero general*, *BAE*, Vol. X, 395-96.

26. Jusepe Antonio González de Salas, *Nueva idea de la tragedia antigua, o ilustración última al libro "De poética" de Aristóteles Stagirita*, segunda edición (Madrid: Antonio de Sánchez, 1778), II, 35.

27. Miguel de Unamuno, "El individualismo español," in *El concepto contemporáneo de España, antología de ensayos [1895-1931]*, eds. Angel del Río y M. J. Benardete (Buenos Aires: Editorial Losada, 1946), p. 105.

28. A. L. Constandse, *Le Baroque espagnol et Calderón de la Barca* (Amsterdam: Boekhandel "Plus Ultra," 1951), pp. 78 ff.

29. Maud Bodkin, *Archetypal Patterns in Poetry* (London: Oxford University Press, 1934), p. 13.

30. The list of plays is bound with an undated seventeenth-century manuscript (No. 16, 977 in the Biblioteca Nacional) of *Numancia cercada*, the only extant version of the play. *Numancia destruída* is preserved in a seventeenth-century *suelta*, the only known copy of which was located in the library of Don Arturo Sedó in Barcelona. I am preparing editions of both plays.

31. For a comparative study of Cervantes' and Rojas' tragedies, see my article "The Numantia Plays of Cervantes and Rojas Zorrilla: the Shift from Collective to Personal Tragedy," *Symposium*, XIV (1960), 100-120.

32. Oscar Mandel, *A Definition of Tragedy* (New York: New York University Press, 1961), p. 107, note 6, calls it the "greatest" of all tragedies with a collective protagonist.

33. Most scholars agree that Cervantes' immediate source was Book VIII of *La corónica general de España. Que continuaua Ambrosio de Morales . . . Prosiguiendo adelante de los cinco libros, que el maestro Florián de Ocampo . . . dexó . . . escritos* (Alcalá de Henares, 1573). Rojas probably used the same work, but he also knew Padre Juan Mariana's *Historia general de España* (original edition in Latin, 1592; first Spanish edition, 1601).

Notes and References

Chapter Four

1. Américo Castro, ed. *Cada qual lo que le toca*, Vol. II of *Teatro Antiguo Español* (Madrid: Hernando, 1917), p. 196.
2. *Ibid.*, p. 246.
3. Cotarelo, *Rojas Zorrilla*, p. 206.
4. *BAE*, III, 451c.
5. Cf. Francisco Bances Candamo, *Theatro de los theatros*, ed. Manuel Serrano y Sanz, in the *Revista de Archivos, Bibliotecas y Museos*, VI (1902), 72.
6. For a study of the influence of the play in other countries, see Arthur Peter, *Des Don Francisco de Rojas Tragödie "Casarse por vengarse" und ihre Bearbeitungen in den anderen Litteraturen* (Dresden: Lehmannsche Buchdruckerei, 1898).
7. A. Valbuena Prat, *Historia de la literatura española* (Barcelona: Editorial Gustavo Gili, 1946), II, 290-91.
8. See Chapter One, note 14.
9. *Comedias escogidas de don Francisco de Rojas Zorrilla* (Madrid: Ortega, 1827), I, 107. Unfortunately, the enthusiastic critic remains anonymous.
10. The sources are studied by Joseph G. Fucilla, "Sobre las fuentes de *Del rey abajo, ninguno*," *Nueva Revista de Filología Hispánica*, V (1951), 381-93. Fucilla was the first to point out that an important source of several incidents in the play is an episode contained in Vicente Espinel's *La vida de Marcos de Obregón* (Madrid, 1618), which occupies all of the *Descanso Sexto* and the first part of *Descanso Séptimo* of the *Relación Tercera*.
11. *Ibid.*, pp. 381-82.
12. Bruce W. Wardropper, "The Poetic World of Rojas Zorrilla's *Del rey abajo, ninguno*," *Romanic Review*, LII (1961), 165-66.
13. This theme is studied by William M. Whitby, "Appearance and Reality in *Del rey abajo, ninguno*," *Hispania*, XLII (1959), 186-91. Other important critical studies include Arnold G. Reichenberger, "Rojas Zorrilla's *Del rey abajo, ninguno* as a Spät-comedia," in *Stil- und Formprobleme in der Literatur*, Vorträge des VII. Kongresses de Internationalen Vereinigung für moderne Sprachen und Literaturen in Heidelberg. Heidelberg, n.d., pp. 194-200; Carlos Ortigoza Vieyra, *Los móviles de la "Comedia" en Lope, Alarcón, Tirso, Moreto, Rojas, Calderón* (México, 1954), pp. 221-28; and the same author's "*Del rey abajo, ninguno*, de Rojas estudiada a través de sus móviles," *Bulletin of the Comediantes*, IX (1957), 1-4.
14. Edición de F. Ruiz Morcuende, Vol. 35 of *Clásicos Castellanos*, tercera edición (Madrid: Espasa-Calpe, 1944), vv. 2501-2502.
15. A. Valbuena Prat, *Historia del teatro español* (Barcelona: Edi-

torial Noguer, 1956), pp. 277-304. The study of *Del rey abajo, ninguno* occupies pp. 290-304.

Chapter Five

1. The standard biography of Lope de Vega in English is H. A. Rennert, *The Life of Lope de Vega* (1562-1635) (New York: G. E. Stechert, 1937), which affords many details on the dramatist's tempestuous life.

2. *Estudios sobre el teatro de Lope de Vega*, ed. Enrique Sánchez Reyes (Santander: Consejo Superior de Investigaciones Científicas, 1949), I, 189.

3. Cotarelo, *Don Francisco de Rojas Zorrilla*, p. 226.

4. *Ibid.*

5. Rojas' use of antiphonal dialogue between Tobías and Sara, punctuated by the angels' comments in duo, may have been suggested by the echo-sonnet in Act II of Lope de Vega's *La historia de Tobías*.

6. Cotarelo, *op. cit.*, pp. 181-87, gives extensive bibliographical information on the collaborative *refundición* of Lope's two-part play.

7. *Ibid.*, p. 189. I have not seen the alleged sources of Rojas' play.

8. For a brief study of the legend and its literary treatments, see Francisco Arquero Soria, *La Virgen de Atocha*, Vol. VIII of *Temas Madrileños* (Madrid: Instituto de Estudios Madrileños, 1954).

9. Gracián Ramírez' killing of his wife and daughters explains the words *segundo Jepté* in the subtitle of the play, although there is little similarity between his deed and Jephte's sacrifice of his daughter, as related in the Book of Judges, xv.

10. Cotarelo, *op. cit.*, p. 202.

11. See Chapter 1, p. 17, and note 3.

12. The criticism of A. Schaeffer, *Geschichte des Spanischen Nationaldramas* (Leipzig, 1890), II, 120 ("a wholly insignificant play") is representative of nineteenth-century opinion of the play. Edward Glaser's study is contained in his *Estudios hispano-portugueses. Relaciones literarias del Siglo de Oro* (Valencia, Editorial Castalia, 1957), Segunda parte, Capítulo II, pp. 179-220.

13. Glaser, *op. cit.*, p. 202, suggests that the source of this episode, known as the *Légende du page de Sainte Elizabeth*, is Fray Marcos de Lisboa, *Parte segunda das chronicas da Ordem dos frades menores . . .* (Lisboa, 1562), fols. 195v.-196v. However, a similar episode, involving a baker who roasts the king's offender alive, is found in Act III of Vélez de Guevara's *De la devoción de la misa*.

14. Extracts from Ribadeneira's book utilized by Rojas are quoted at length in my edition of the play, in Vol. 153 of *Clásicos Castellanos* (Madrid: Espasa-Calpe, 1961). All citations are to this edition.

Notes and References

15. Cf. Ribadeneira, *op. cit.*, I, fol. 368.
16. Ed. MacCurdy, *op. cit.*, Act II, p. 170.
17. *Ibid.*, Act III, pp. 203-4. Here is a translation of the passage: "*B.* I haven't seen a more importunate sun. *A.* Go, go, for I hear steps in the antechamber. *B.* No, it is only the wind stirring there; sleep for a while, my lady. *A.* Since you order me to do so, I'll not try to avoid it, although I must fall asleep in your arms . . . *B.* Rest and sleep, serene eyes. *A.* Are you there? *B.* I want to leave you buried in peaceful sleep. *A.* I'll sleep to please you, although I won't really sleep because I am dying of love which is sleep of another kind, a glorious suffering and a sweet death. *B.* Sleep, sleep. *A.* I entrust my life into your hands. *B.* She has gone to sleep peacefully. *A.* [In her sleep] Go, my love . . . *B.* Rest and sleep, serene eyes. *A.* Where am I?"
18. Cotarelo, *op. cit.*, p. 211.
19. *Ibid.*, p. 68.
20. Cf. Valbuena Prat, *Historia de la literatura española* (Barcelona: Editorial Gustavo Gili, 1946), II, 300.
21. Emilio Cotarelo y Mori, *Mira de Amescua y su teatro. Estudio biográfico y crítico* (Madrid: Tip. de la *Revista de Archivos*, 1931), p. 89.
22. In Vol. II of *Teatro Antiguo Español* (Madrid: Hernando, 1917).
23. *Famoso Auto Sacramental del Gran Patio de Palacio*, in *Autos sacramentales, con cuatro comedias nuevas, y sus loas, y entremeses. Primera parte* (Madrid: María de Quiñones, 1655), p. 55.

Chapter Six

1. Marcelino Menéndez Pelayo, *Estudios sobre el teatro de Lope de Vega*, VI, 367-68.
2. *Ibid.*, p. 368.
3. *Ibid.*
4. Cotarelo, *op. cit.*, p. 159.
5. S. G. Morley and C. Bruerton, *The Chronology of Lope de Vega's "comedias,"* p. 265: "We cannot be sure . . . that it is his [Lope's]."
6. Cotarelo, *op. cit.*, p. 159.
7. One Ms. is in the Biblioteca Nacional (No. 16711), the other in the Biblioteca Municipal (Madrid).
8. Cotarelo, *op. cit.*, pp. 208-9.
9. Morley and Bruerton, *op. cit.*, p. 182.
10. Cotarelo, *op. cit.*, pp. 144-45.
11. Lope's source was the ninth of Matteo Bandello's *novelle*, available in two editions of a Spanish translation, *Historias trágicas exemplares sacadas de las obras del Bandello Veronés* (Salamanca, 1589;

Valladolid, 1603), based in turn on the French translation of Bandello made by Pierres Boisteau and François Belleforest (1559).

12. A. A. Parker, *The Approach to the Spanish Drama of the Golden Age* (London: The Hispanic and Luso-Brazilian Councils, 1957), pp. 9-10.

Chapter Seven

1. H. A. Rennert, *The Spanish Stage in the Time of Lope de Vega* (New York: G. E. Stechert, 1909), p. 276.

2. *Ibid.*

3. Juana de José Prades, *Teoría sobre los personajes de la Comedia Nueva* (Madrid: Consejo Superior de Investigaciones Científicas, 1963), has studied the stock characters (*dama, galán, gracioso, criada, rey* and *padre*) in the plays of five lesser known contemporaries of Lope de Vega, and concludes that there was an unwritten but almost unalterable precept concerning them, a precept as rigidly observed by Spanish dramatists as Aristotle's precepts were observed by neoclassicists: "¿Qué precepto hay más rígido que emplear *siempre los mismos seis personajes?* ¿Qué canon más riguroso que conformarlos siempre *con unos mismos atributos?*" (p. 254).

4. For a schematic outline of the plot of the cape-and-sword plays and their distribution of characters, see Dámaso Alonso y Carlos Bousoño, *Seis calas en la expresión literaria española* (Madrid: Editorial Gredos, 1951), p. 176.

5. Rojas' play was first performed on January 29, 1637, but is believed to have been composed in 1635 or 1636. Calderón's play, *El alcaide de sí mismo* (believed to have been written in 1636), also involves a master and servant who change roles, but this incident is relatively unimportant.

6. Adolph von Schack, *Historia de la literatura y del arte dramático en España*, traducida . . . por Eduardo de Mier (Madrid: Imprenta y Fundición de M. Tello, 1887), V, 86-87.

7. See my article, "The Spanish Sources of Paul Scarron's *Jodolet duelliste*," in *Hispanic Studies in Honor of Nicholson B. Adams*, ed. John E. Keller and Karl-Ludwig Selig (Chapel Hill: The University of North Carolina Press, 1965), pp. 107-11.

8. Cotarelo, *op. cit.*, p. 198.

9. *Ibid.*, p. 204.

10. This play has been attributed to Lope de Vega and to Calderón, but E. Juliá Martínez, ed. *Obras de don Guillén de Castro y Bellvís* (Madrid: Imp. de la *Revista de Archivos, Bibliotecas y Museos*, 1926), II, xxi, accepts it as Guillén de Castro's.

11. *BAE*, I, 63c-64a.

Notes and References

12. Cotarelo, *op. cit.*, p. 205.
13. *The Relation of Moreto's "El desdén con el desdén" to Suggested Sources*, in *Indiana University Studies*, Vol. XI, Study No. 62 (Bloomington: Indiana University Press, 1924), pp. 73-79.
14. *Ibid.*, p. 75.
15. *BAE*, II. 306c-307a.

Chapter Eight

1. George Ticknor, *op. cit.*, II, 244.
2. Carlos Ortigoza Vieyra, *Los móviles de la "comedia" en Lope, Alarcón, Tirso, Moreto, Rojas, Calderón* (Mexico: C. U., 1954), p. 203, note.
3. For a good introduction to the *comedia de figurón*, see Edwin B. Place, "Notes on the Grotesque: the *comedia de figurón* at Home and Abroad," *Publications of the Modern Language Association*, LIV (1939), 412-31.
4. For more on the role of the bathing nude, see my note "The Bathing Nude in Golden Age Drama," *Romance Notes*, I (1959), 1-4.

Chapter Nine

1. Cf. Albert E. Sloman, *The Dramatic Craftsmanship of Calderón* (Oxford, 1958), in which eight of Calderón's recasts are compared in detail with their source-plays.
2. Cotarelo, *op. cit.*, p. 119.
3. Cf. Angel Valbuena, *Literatura dramática española*, p. 259.
4. H. Petriconi, "El tema de Lucrecia y Virginia," *Clavileño*, Año II, Núm. 8 (Marzo-Abril, 1951), 5.
5. Brenan, *The Literature of the Spanish People*, p. 313.

Selected Bibliography

PRIMARY SOURCES

Editions of Rojas' Plays

In this section are listed: (1) the first known edition of the thirty-six plays and the *autos sacramentales* included in this study, and (2) an accessible modern edition, when existent, to which citations are usually made in the course of the study. Omitted are apochryphal plays and those written in collaboration.

Abre el ojo, in *Parte I;* also in *BAE,* Vol. LIV, pp. 123-45.
Los acreedores del hombre (auto sacramental). Ms. in the *BN* (No. 15168).
Los áspides de Cleopatra, in *Parte II;* also in *BAE,* Vol. LIV, pp. 421-40.
Los bandos de Verona, in *Parte II;* also in *BAE,* Vol. LIV, pp. 367-88.
Cada qual lo que le toca. Edición de Américo Castro. Vol. II of *Teatro Antiguo Español.* (Madrid: Hernando, 1917).
El Caín de Cataluña, in *El mejor de los mejores libros de comedias . . .* Alcalá, 1651; Madrid, 1653. Also in *BAE,* Vol. LIV, pp. 271-94.
Casarse por vengarse, in *Parte XXIX* of *Comedias de diferentes autores* (attributed here to Calderón), Valencia, 1636; also in *Parte XXX* of *Comedias famosas de varios autores,* Zaragoza, 1636; also in *BAE,* Vol. LIV, pp. 103-22.
Los celos de Rodamonte, in *Parte I.* Not modernly reprinted.
Del rey abajo, ninguno, in *Parte XLII* of *Comedias de diferentes autores* (attributed here to Calderón), Zaragoza, 1650; edición de F. Ruiz Morcuende, Vol. 35 of *Clásicos Castellanos.* Tercera edición. (Madrid: Espasa-Calpe, 1944).
El desafío de Carlos Quinto, printed as a *suelta* without place or date; also in *BAE,* Vol. LIV, pp. 407-20.
Donde ay agravios no ay zelos, in *Parte I;* also in *BAE,* Vol. LIV, pp. 147-68.
Los encantos de Medea, in *Parte II.* Not modernly reprinted.
Entre bobos anda el juego, in *Parte II;* edición de F. Ruiz Morcuende,

Vol. 35 of *Clásicos Castellanos*. Tercera edición. (Madrid: Espasa-Calpe, 1944).

Galán, discreto y valiente (*auto sacramental*), in *Autos sacramentales, con cuatro comedias nuevas, y sus loas, y entremeses. Primera parte.* (Madrid: María de Quiñones, 1655). (Hereafter referred to as *Parte I de Autos sacramentales.*)

El gran patio de palacio (*auto sacramental*), in *Parte I de Autos sacramentales.*

Hércules (*auto sacramental*). Ms. in the Archivo Municipal de Madrid (Legajo 16-3-470).

Lo que quería ver el Marqués de Villena, in *Parte II;* also in *BAE,* Vol. LIV, pp. 349-66.

Lo que son mugeres, in *Parte II;* also in *BAE,* Vol. LIV, pp. 191-211.

Lucrecia y Tarquino, printed as a *suelta* without place or date. Edited by Raymond R. MacCurdy. (Albuquerque: The University of New Mexico Press, 1963).

El más impropio verdugo por la más justa venganza, in *Parte II;* also in *BAE,* Vol. LIV, pp. 169-90.

El mejor amigo el muerto (*y capuchino escocés*). Ms. in the *BN* (No. 15671).

Morir pensando matar, in *Parte XXXIII* of *Doce comedias famosas de varios autores* . . . Valencia, 1642. Edited by Raymond R. MacCurdy, Vol. 153 of *Clásicos Castellanos.* (Madrid: Espasa-Calpe, 1961).

No ay amigo para amigo, in *Parte I;* also in *BAE,* Vol. LIV, pp. 83-102.

No hay duelo entre dos amigos, printed as a *suelta* without place or date. Not modernly reprinted.

No hay ser padre siendo rey, in *Parte I;* also in *BAE,* Vol. LIV, pp. 389-406.

Nuestra Señora de Atocha, in *Parte II;* also in *BAE,* Vol. LIV, pp. 471-92.

Numancia cercada. Ms. in the *BN* (No. 16977).

Numancia destruída, printed as a *suelta* without place or date. Not modernly reprinted.

Obligados y ofendidos, in *Parte I;* also in *BAE,* Vol. LIV, pp. 61-82.

Peligrar en los remedios, in *Parte I;* also in *BAE,* Vol. LIV, pp. 349-66.

Persiles y Segismunda, in *Parte XXIX* of *Comedias de diferentes autores,* Valencia, 1636; also in *Parte XXX* of *Comedias famosas de varios autores,* Zaragoza, 1636; also in Rojas' *Parte I.* Not modernly reprinted.

El primer Marqués de Astorga. Ms. in the *BN* (No. 16711).

Primero es la honra que el gusto, printed as a *suelta* (Madrid: Impr. de Juan Sanz, n. d.). Also in *BAE,* Vol. LIV, pp. 441-52.

El Profeta falso Mahoma, in *Parte I.* Not modernly reprinted.

Selected Bibliography

Progne y Filomena, in *Parte I*; also in *BAE*, Vol. LIV, pp. 39-60.

El rico avariento (auto sacramental). Two mss. in the *BN* (Nos. 15150 and 15266).

Santa Isabel, Reina de Portugal, in *Parte I*; also in *BAE*, Vol. LIV, pp. 255-69.

Sin honra no ay amistad, in *Parte II*; also in *BAE*, Vol. LIV, pp. 295-318.

Los trabajos de Tobías, in *Parte XXXIII* of *Comedias de diferentes autores*, Valencia, 1642; also in Rojas' *Parte II*. Not modernly reprinted.

La traición busca el castigo, in *Parte I*; also in *BAE*, Vol. LIV, pp. 233-54.

La vida en el ataúd, in *Parte XXXII* of *Comedias escogidas de los mejores ingenios de España*, Madrid, 1669. Edited by Raymond R. MacCurdy, Vol. 153 of *Clásicos Castellanos*. (Madrid: Espasa-Calpe, 1961).

La viña de Nabot (auto sacramental). Edición de Américo Castro. Vol. II of *Teatro Antiguo Español* (Madrid: Hernando, 1917).

SECONDARY SOURCES

Other Works Cited

Academia burlesca en Buen Retiro a la Magestad de Philippo IV el Grande. Edición de Antonio Pérez Gómez (Valencia: Tip. Moderna, 1952).

Alonso, Dámaso, y Bousoño, Carlos. *Seis calas en la expresión literaria española*. (Madrid: Editorial Gredos, 1951).

Aristotle. *On the Art of Poetry*. Translated by S. H. Butcher. (New York: The Liberal Arts Press, 1948).

Arquero Soria, Francisco. *La Virgen de Atocha*. Temas Madrileños, Núm. VIII. (Madrid: Instituto de Estudios Madrileños, 1954).

Bances Candamo, Francisco A. *Theatro de los theatros . . .* Edición de Manuel Serrano y Sanz. In *Revista de Archivos, Bibliotecas y Museos* (3ª época), V (1901), 155 ff.; VI (1902), 73 ff.

Barrera y Leirado, Cayetano Alberto de la. *Catálogo bibliográfico y biográfico del teatro antiguo español, desde sus orígenes hasta mediados del siglo XVIII* (Madrid: M. Rivadeneyra, 1860).

Bodkin, Maud. *Archetypal Patterns in Poetry*. (London: Oxford University Press, 1948).

Bowers, Fredson Thayer. *Elizabethan Revenge Tragedy, 1587-1642*. (Princeton: Princeton University Press, 1940).

Brenan, Gerald. *The Literature of the Spanish People*. (New York: Meridian Books, 1957).

Cáncer, Jerónimo. *Loa sacramental*. In *Autos sacramentales, con cuatro comedias nuevas, y sus loas, y entremeses. Primera parte*. (Madrid: María de Quiñones, 1655).

Castro, Américo (ed.). Francisco de Rojas Zorrilla, *Cada qual lo que le toca* y *La viña de Nabot*. Vol. II of Teatro Antiguo Español. (Madrid: Hernando, 1917).

———. "Obras mal atribuídas a Rojas Zorrilla," *Revista de Filología Española*, III (1916), 66-68.

Chaytor, H. J. *Dramatic Theory in Spain*. (Cambridge: The University Press, 1925).

Constandse, A. L. *Le Baroque espagnol et Calderón de la Barca*. (Amsterdam: Boekhandel "Plus Ultra," 1951).

Cotarelo y Mori, Emilio. *Don Francisco de Rojas Zorrilla, noticias biográficas y biliográficas*. (Madrid: Imprenta de la Revista de Archivos, 1911).

———. *Mira de Amescua y su teatro. Estudio biográfico y crítico*. (Madrid: Tipografía de la Revista de Archivos, 1931).

Cotarelo y Valledor, Armando. *El teatro de Cervantes*. (Madrid: Tip. de la Revista de Archivos, Bibliotecas y Museos, 1915).

Croce, Benedetto. *Storia dell Età barocca in Italia*. (Bari: Laterza and Figli, 1957).

Cruzada Villaamil, G. "Teatro antiguo español: datos inéditos que dan a conocer la cronología de las comedias representadas en el reinado de Felipe IV en los sitios reales, etc.," in *El Averiguador*, Madrid, 1871, I, 7-11, 25-27, 73-75, 106-8, 123-25, 170-72, 201-2.

Duis, Dorothy L. "Versification in the *comedias* of Rojas Zorrilla." Unpublished Master's thesis, Ohio State University, 1926.

Entrambasaguas, Joaquín de. "La leyenda de Rosamunda," *Revista Bibliográfica y Documental*, II (1949), 339-89.

———. "Una guerra literaria del Siglo de Oro: Lope de Vega y los preceptistas aristotélicos," *Boletín de la Real Academia Española*," XIX (1932), 135-60, 260-326; XX (1933), 405-44, 569-600, 687-734; XXI (1934), 82-112, 238-72, 423-62, 587-628, 795-857.

Escribano, F. S. "Cuatro contribuciones españolas a la preceptiva dramática mundial," *Bulletin of the Comediantes*, XIII (Spring, 1961), 1-3.

Fucilla, Joseph G. "Sobre las fuentes de *Del rey abajo, ninguno*," *Nueva Revista de Filología Hispánica*, V (1951), 381-93.

Gillet, Joseph E. "A Note on the Tragic *Admiratio*," *Modern Language Review*, XIII (1918), 233-38.

———. "Lucrecia—necia," *Hispanic Review*, XV (1947), 120-36.

Glaser, Edward. *Estudios hispano-portugueses. Relaciones literarias del Siglo de Oro*. (Valencia: Editorial Castalia, 1957).

Selected Bibliography

González de Salas, Jusepe Antonio. *Nueva idea de la tragedia antigua, o ilustración última al libro singular "De poética" de Aristóteles Stagirita, Primera parte. Tragedia práctica, observaciones que deben preceder a la tragedia española intitulada "Las Troianas" Segunda parte.* Segunda edición, 2 vols. (Madrid: Por D. Antonio de Sancha, 1778).

Harlan, Mabel M. *The Relation of Moreto's "El desdén con el desdén" to Suggested Sources.* Indiana University Studies, No. 62, Vol. XI. (Bloomington: Indiana University Press, 1924).

Hilborn, Harry W. *A Chronology of the Plays of D. Pedro Calderón de la Barca.* (Toronto: The University of Toronto Press, 1938).

Hurtado y J. de la Serna, Juan, y González Palencia, Angel. *Historia de la literatura española.* Quinta edición. (Madrid: SAETA, 1943).

José Prades, Juana de. *Teoría sobre los personajes de la Comedia Nueva.* (Madrid: Consejo Superior de Investigaciones Científicas, 1963).

Juliá Martínez, Eduardo (ed.). *Obras de don Guillén de Castro y Bellvís.* 3 vols. (Madrid: Imp. de la *Revista de Archivos, Bibliotecas y Museos,* 1925).

——. *Poetas dramáticos valencianos.* 2 vols. (Madrid: Tip. de la *Revista de Archivos,* 1929).

Lancaster, Henry Carrington. *A History of French Dramatic Literature in the Seventeenth Century.* Part II, Vol. II. (Baltimore: The Johns Hopkins University Press, 1929).

——. "The Ultimate Source of Rotrou's *Venceslas* and of Rojas Zorrilla's *No hay ser padre siendo rey,*" *Modern Philology,* XV (1917-1918), 435-40.

Lista y Aragón, Alberto. *Ensayos literarios y críticos.* 2 vols. in one. (Seville: Calvo-Rubio, 1844).

MacCurdy, Raymond R. "Francisco de Rojas Zorrilla," *Bulletin of the Comediantes,* IX (Spring, 1957), 7-9.

——. *Francisco de Rojas Zorrilla and the Tragedy.* University of New Mexico Publications in Language and Literature, No. 13. (Albuquerque: University of New Mexico Press, 1958); reprinted, 1966.

——. "The Numantia Plays of Cervantes and Rojas Zorrilla: the Shift from Collective to Personal Tragedy," *Symposium,* XIV (1960), 100-120.

——. (ed.). Francisco de Rojas Zorrilla, *Lucrecia y Tarquino.* Together with a Transcription of Agustín Moreto y Cabaña, *Baile de Lucrecia y Tarquino.* (Albuquerque: The University of New Mexico Press, 1963).

——. *Francisco de Rojas Zorrilla: bibliografía crítica.* Cuadernos Bibliográficos, Vol. 18. (Madrid: Consejo Superior de Investigaciones Científicas, 1965).

——. "The Spanish Sources of Paul Scarron's *Jodolet duelliste*." In *Hispanic Studies in Honor of Nicholson B. Adams*. University of North Carolina Studies in the Romance Languages and Literatures, No. 59. (Chapel Hill: The University of North Carolina Press, 1966).

——. "The Bathing Nude in Golden Age Drama," *Romance Notes*, I (1959), 1-4.

Malvezzi, Virgilio. *Tarquino el Soberbio ... Traduzido del Toscano ... [por] Don Francisco Bolle Pintaflor*. (Madrid: Imprenta del Reyno, 1635).

——. *Romvlvs and Tarquin, Written in Italian by the Marques Virgilio Malvezzi. And now taught English by Henry Earle of Monmouth*. 3rd. ed. London: 1648.

Mandel, Oscar. *A Definition of Tragedy*. (New York: New York University Press, 1961).

Marañón, Gregorio. *El Conde-Duque de Olivares*. (Madrid: Espasa-Calpe, 1936).

Medel del Castillo, Francisco. *Indice general alfabético de todos los títulos de comedias que se han escrito por varios autores antiguos y modernos ...* Edited by J. M. Hill. In *Revue Hispanique*, LXXV (1929), 144-369.

Menéndez Pelayo, Marcelino. *Estudios y discursos de crítica histórica y literaria*. Edición de Enrique Sánchez Reyes. 7 vols. (Santander: Consejo Superior de Investigaciones Científicas, 1941).

——. *Estudios sobre el teatro de Lope de Vega*. Edición de Enrique Sánchez Reyes. 6 vols. (Santander: Consejo Superior de Investigaciones Científicas, 1949).

Mesonero Romanos, Ramón de. "Apuntes biográficos, bibliográficos y críticos de don Francisco de Rojas Zorrilla," in *Comedias escogidas de ... Rojas*. Vol. LIV of *BAE*. (Madrid: M. Rivadeneyra, 1866).

Morby, Edwin S. "The Influence of Senecan Tragedy in the Plays of Juan de la Cueva," *Studies in Philology*, XXXIV (1937), 383-91.

——. "Some Observations on 'tragedia' and 'tragicomedia' in Lope," *Hispanic Review*, XI (1943), 185-209.

Morley, S. Griswold, and Bruerton, Courtney. *The Chronology of Lope de Vega's "Comedias."* (New York: The Modern Language Association of America, 1940).

Ochoa, Eugenio de (ed.). *Tesoro del teatro español*. 5 vols. (Paris: Baudry, 1838).

Ortigoza Vieyra, Carlos. *Los móviles de la "comedia" en Lope, Alarcón, Tirso, Moreto, Rojas, Calderón*. (México: C. U., 1954).

——. "*Del rey abajo, ninguno*, de Rojas estudiada a través de sus móviles," *Bulletin of the Comediantes*, IX (1957), 1-4.

Selected Bibliography

Ovid (Publius Ovidius Naso). *Metamorphoses*. Translated by Rolfe Humphries. (Bloomington: Indiana University Press, 1957).

Parker, A. A. *The Approach to the Spanish Drama of the Golden Age*. (London: The Hispanic and Luso-Brazilian Councils, 1957).

Paz y Melia, Antonio (ed.). *Sales españolas*. Segunda serie. (Madrid: Imp. de la *Revista de Archivos*, 1902).

Pellicer, Casiano. *Tratado histórico sobre el origen y progresos de la comedia y del histrionismo en España*. 2 vols. in one. (Madrid: Imprenta de la Administración del Real Arbitrio de Beneficencia, 1804).

Pellicer de Tovar, José. *Anfiteatro de Felipe el Grande*. (Madrid: Por Juan González, 1631).

Pérez de Montalván, Juan. *Para todos, exemplos morales, humanos, y divinos* . . . (Sevilla: Imprenta . . . de los Gómez, 1736).

Peter, Arthur. *Des Don Francisco de Rojas Tragödie "Casarse por vengarse" und ihre Bearbeitungen in den anderen Litteraturen*. (Dresden: Lehmannsche Buchdruckerei, 1898).

Petriconi, H. "El tema de Lucrecia y Virginia," *Clavileño*, Año II, Núm. 8 (Marzo-Abril, 1951), 1-5.

Pfandl, Ludwig. *Historia de la literatura nacional española en la edad de oro*. Traducción por J. R. Balaguer. Segunda edición. (Barcelona: Editorial Gustavo Gili, 1952).

Place, Edwin B. "Notes on the Grostesque: the *comedia de figurón* at Home and Abroad," *Publications of the Modern Language Association*, LIV (1939), 412-21.

Reichenberger, Arnold G. "Rojas Zorrilla's *Del rey abajo, ninguno* as a Spät-comedia." In *Stil-und Formprobleme in der Literature*, Vorträge des VII. Kongresses der Internationalen Vereinigung für moderne Sprachen und Literaturn in Heidelberg. Heidelberg: n.d. Pp. 194-200.

Rennert, Hugo A. *The Spanish Stage in the Time of Lope de Vega*. (New York: The Hispanic Society of America, 1909).

——. *The Life of Lope de Vega* (1562-1635). (New York: G. E. Stechert, 1937).

Ribadeneira, Pedro de. *Flos Sanctorum, o Libro de las vidas de los santos*. (Barcelona: Sebastián Cormella, 1623).

Rojas, Fray Francisco de. *Apologías trágicas. Primera, y segunda parte*. No place: 1654.

Sáinz de Robles, Francisco Carlos. *El teatro español, historia y antología*. 7 vols. (Madrid: Aguilar, 1943).

Schack, A. F. von. *Historia de la literatura y el arte dramático en España*. Traducida por E. de Mier. 5 vols. (Madrid: Imprenta y Fundición de M. Tello, 1885-1887).

Schaeffer, Adolph. *Geschichte des Spanischen Nationaldramas*. 2 vols. (Leipzig: F. A. Brockhaus, 1890).

Seneca, Lucius Annaeus. *Of a Happy Life*. In *Latin Literature in Translation*. Edited by Kevin Guinagh and Alfred P. Dorjahn. (New York: Longmans, Green and Co., 1950).

Serrano y Sanz, Manuel (ed.). *Vejamen* [de 1637]. En el apéndice de Luis Vélez de Guevara, *El diablo cojuelo*. Edición de A. Bonilla y San Martín. (Vigo: Librería de Eugenio Krapf, 1902).

Shakespeare, William. *The Rape of Lucrece*. In *The Poems*. Edited by J. C. Maxwell. (Cambridge: At the University Press, 1966).

———. *Othello*. In *Twenty-three Plays and the Sonnets*. Edited by T. M. Parrott. Revised edition. (New York: Charles Scribner's Sons, 1953).

Suárez de Figueroa, Cristóbal. *El Passagero. Advertencias vtilisimas a la vida hvmana*. (Madrid: Por Luis Sánchez, 1617).

Ticknor, George. *History of Spanish Literature*. 4th ed., 3 vols. (Boston: James R. Osgood and Co., 1872).

Unamuno, Miguel de. "El individualismo español," in *El concepto contemporáneo de España, antología de ensayos (1895-1931)*. Edición de Angel del Río y M. J. Benardete. (Buenos Aires: Editorial Losada, 1946).

Valbuena Prat, Angel. *Historia de la literatura española*. Segunda edición, 2 vols. (Barcelona: Editorial Gustavo Gili, 1946).

———. *Literatura dramática española*. (Barcelona: Editorial Labor, 1930).

———. *Historia del teatro español*. (Barcelona: Editorial Noguer, 1956).

Vega Carpio, Lope de. *El castigo sin venganza*. Edición de C. F. Adolfo Van Dam. (Groningen: P. Noordhoff, 1928).

Wardropper, Bruce W. "The Poetic World of Rojas Zorrilla's *Del rey abajo, ninguno*," *Romanic Review*, LII (1961), 161-72.

Whitby, William M. "Appearance and Reality in *Del rey abajo, ninguno*," *Hispania*, XLII (1959), 186-91.

Wittman, Brigitte (ed.) *Donde ay agravios no ay zelos* von Francisco de Rojas Zorrilla. Kölner Romanistische Arbeiten, Neue Folge-Heft 26. (Genève-Paris: Droz-Minard, 1962).

A LIST OF SUGGESTED READINGS

In this section are listed the titles of a few books which contain valuable information concerning Rojas' life and works. They include (1) editions of his plays that have useful introductions, (2) monographs and general studies devoted to him, and (3) the titles of a few histories of Spanish drama and literature which contain especially good sections on Rojas. Most of these books have been cited during

Selected Bibliography

the course of this study and are listed in Section II of the Bibliography. Articles and essays will not be listed in this section.

Castro, Américo (ed.). Francisco de Rojas Zorrilla, *Cada qual lo que le toca* y *La viña de Nabot*. Vol. II of *Teatro Antiguo Español*. (Madrid: Hernando, 1917). Castro's study of the "valor literario" of *Cada cual* (pp. 183-97) and his "Resumen" (pp. 245-48) offer a perceptive analysis of Rojas' treatment of conjugal honor and of his alleged feminist ideas.

Cotarelo y Mori, Emilio. *Don Francisco de Rojas Zorrilla, noticias biográficas y bibliográficas*. (Madrid: Imprenta de la *Revista de Archivos*, 1911). Although published more than half a century ago, Cotarelo's book remains the fundamental work concerning Rojas' biography and the dates of the performance of his plays. Much of the bibliographical information is out-of-date, and the criticism is meager.

Gouldson, Kathleen. "Religion and Superstition in the Plays of Rojas Zorrilla" and "Rojas Zorrilla and Seventeenth-Century Spain." In *Three Studies in Golden Age Drama* (*Spanish Golden Age Poetry and Drama*). Liverpool Studies in Spanish Literature: second series. Edited by E. Allison Peers. (Liverpool: Institute of Hispanic Studies, 1946). Pp. 89-118. In addition to the contents indicated by the title, the first study considers the omens occurring in Rojas' plays. The second study concerns social and political institutions as reflected in the plays.

MacCurdy, Raymond R. *Francisco de Rojas Zorrilla: bibliografía crítica*. Cuadernos Bibliográficos, Vol. 18. (Madrid: Consejo Superior de Investigaciones Científicas, 1965). The bibliography contains the following major sections: (1) general catalogue of Rojas' works, (2) manuscripts, (3) special collections of Rojas' plays, (4) Rojas' plays in general collections, (5) editions and *sueltas*, (6) influences (Spanish *refundiciones* and foreign translations and adaptations), (7) studies (includes biographical and bibliographical studies, general studies and monographs, and studies devoted to individual plays).

———. *Francisco de Rojas Zorrilla and the Tragedy*. University of New Mexico Publications in Language and Literature, No. 13. (Albuquerque: University of New Mexico Press, 1958). Contains the following chapters: A Biographical Sketch, Spanish Tragedy Before Rojas, Rojas' Tragedies: Theme and Story, Characters, Technique and Art, Conception and Fulfillment, Conclusion.

Ortigoza Vieyra, Carlos. *Los móviles de la "comedia" en Lope, Alarcón, Tirso, Moreto, Rojas, Calderón*. (México: C. U., 1954). Chapter

VII (pp. 177-229), devoted to Rojas, contains many perceptive observations on a large number of his plays.

Ruiz Morcuende, F. (ed.). *Francisco de Rojas, Teatro (Del rey abajo, ninguno y Entre bobos anda el juego)*. Vol. 35 of *Clásicos Castellanos*. Tercera edición. (Madrid: Espasa-Calpe, 1944). The *prólogo* (pp. IX-LII) includes a biographical section, a bibliographical section (largely out-of-date), a summary of critical opinion on Rojas, and brief critical remarks on the two plays edited in the volume.

Schmidt, Gisela. *Studien zu den Komödien des Don Francisco de Rojas Zorrilla*. Inaugural Dissertation zur Erlangung des Doktorgrades der Philosophischen Fakultät der Universität Köln. Köln: Romanisches Seminar der Universität Köln, 1959. This study, arranged topically, considers such matters as Rojas' treatment of honor, feminism, characters, comic elements (including long sections on the *gracioso* and *figurón*), representation of Spanish society, structure of the plays, and dramatic technique and devices.

Valbuena (Prat), Angel. *Literatura dramática española*. (Barcelona: Colección Labor, 1930). Pp. 249-60. A succinct but perceptive appraisal of Rojas' originality, including his penchant for tragedy and, at the same time, his strong comic verve. Contains a classification of some of the major plays.

——. *Historia de la literatura española*. Segunda edición. (Barcelona: Editorial Gustavo Gili, 1946). Vol. II, pp. 287-302. Contains the following sections: "Francisco de Rojas y su época. Evolución del sentimiento del honor y del deber"; "Rojas, poeta trágico"; "Los caracteres, las formas cómicas, el realismo"; "Los autos de Rojas." The treatment of Rojas' *autos sacramentales,* although necessarily brief and incomplete, is the best thing in print on the subject.

Index

abbreviations, 8, 141
(*El*) *Abencerraje*, 86, 106
Abre (*Abrir*) *el ojo*, 16, 29, 35, 126, 127-129
(*Los*) *Acreedores del hombre*, 32, 93
adaptations of Rojas' plays, 5-6, 73-74, 112, 117, 121, 139
Agamemnon (Seneca), 52
(*El*) *alcalde Ardite*, 32
allegorical characters, 61, 62, 64, 94, 95
Alonso, Dámaso, 150, 155
(*Los*) *amantes de Verona* (Cristóbal de Rozas), 106, 108
Amar después de la muerte (Calderón), 121
(*El*) *amo criado* (Hartzenbusch), 112
Amphitheater of Philip the Great, 16
An Insult Can Also Be Poisonous, 32
Añasco de Talavera (Cubillo de Aragón), 119
Anfiteatro de Felipe el Grande, 16
Antony, 5
Antony and Cleopatra (Shakespeare), 39
Apologético de las comedias españolas (Ricardo de Turia), 37
Aremberg, Carlos de, 83
Argensola, Lupercio Leonardo de, 52-53
Ariosto, Ludovico, 100, 103
Aristotle, 37, 47, 145, 150, 155

Arquero Soria, Francisco, 142, 148, 155
Arte nuevo de hacer comedias en este tiempo (Lope de Vega), 36
(*Los*) *áspides de Cleopatra*, 5, 28, 29, 34, 38, 39-42
Atreus, 50
authentic plays, 8, 25-32
auto sacramental, 8, 20, 22, 23, 29, 32, 35, 93-99, 106, 138
Autos sacramentales con cuatro comedias nuevas y sus loas y entremeses, 94, 95
Avisos, 20

Balaguer, J. R., 143
(Prince) Baltasar Carlos, 22, 97
(*La*) *Baltasara*, 17, 31
Bances Candamo, Francisco, 147, 155
Bandello, Matteo, 107, 149, 150
(*The*) *Bandit Solposto*, 31
(*El*) *Bandolero Solposto*, 31
(*Los*) *bandos de Verona*, 5, 21, 29, 35, 100, 103, 106-109, 138
baroque, 33, 34, 43, 60, 61, 91
Barrera y Leirado, Cayetano Alberto de la, 38, 144, 155
Batres, Alfonso de, 19, 20
bathing nude, 131, 134, 151
beatus ille, 77
Belmonte, Luis de, 31
Below the King All Men Are Peers, 6, 29, 75-79
biography, 15-23
Bezón, Francisca, 21, 142

Bezón, Juan, 21, 142
biblical references, 55, 73
biblical sources, 80, 93, 94, 96
Biblioteca de Autores Españoles,
104, 141, 143
Bodkin, Maud, 146, 155
Boisrobert, François Le Metel de,
121
Bolle Pintaflor, Francisco, 43
Bonilla, A., 142
Book of Tobias, 80
Borbón, Isabel de, 18, 20, 22
Borbón, María de (Princess of
Carignan), 18
Bousoño, Carlos, 150, 155
Bowers, Fredson, T., 145, 155
Brenan, Gerald, 127, 140, 151, 155
Bruerton, C., 143, 149
Bryan, (Sir) Francis, 78
Buen Retiro, 21, 106, 109
(The) Burial of Count Orgaz (El
Greco), 15
burlesque, 114, 131, 133, 140
*(Las) cabezas de los siete infantes
de Lara,* 139

Cada cual lo que le toca, 27, 29, 35,
66, 68, 70-71, 137, 139
Cain and Abel plays, 56-61
(El) Caín de Cataluña, 28, 29, 34,
56, 57-58, 61
(The) Cain of Catalonia, 28, 29,
57-58
Calderón de la Barca, José, 15
Calderón de la Barca, Pedro, 6, 11,
15, 17, 20, 22, 25, 28, 31, 33, 38,
57, 60, 69, 74, 75, 80, 93, 121,
135, 136, 137, 142, 150, 151
*(Las) canas en el papel y dudoso en
la venganza* (Guillén de Castro),
118
Cáncer, Jerónimo, 23, 31, 97, 156
cape-and-sword plays, 34, 35, 63,
75, 110-125, 128, 132, 134
(La) cárcel del mundo (Antonio
Coello), 93
caricature, 127, 133

Carillo, (Fray) Juan, 87
Casarse por vengarse, 28, 29, 35, 66,
72, 73-75
Cascales, Francisco, 37
Castelvines y Monteses (Lope de
Vega), 106, 107
catharis, 52, 64
(El) castigo sin venganza (Lope de
Vega), 37, 135
Castillo Solórzano, Alonso de, 39,
132-133
Castro, Américo, 67, 96, 143, 147,
160
Castro, Guillén de, 48, 49, 50, 56,
57, 73, 118, 150
Catalán (El) Serrallonga, 31
(La) Celestina (Fernando de Ro-
jas), 6
(Los) celos de Rodamonte, 30, 35,
100, 103-104
(El) celoso prudente (Tirso de Mo-
lina), 77
*(El) cerco de Viena y socorro por
Carlos V* (Lope de Vega), 104
Cervantes, 11, 15, 17, 18, 61, 62, 63,
64, 65, 84, 100, 101, 119, 130,
146
Chaytor, H. J., 144, 156
Chiriboga, 22, 143
chivalresque plays, 33
classical dramaturgy, 36, 37, 83, 135
classical themes, 39-52
classical tragedy, 37, 38, 39
classification, 32-35
Cleopatra, 5, 39, 40, 41, 42
Cleopatra's Serpents, 28, 29, 39-42
Coello, Antonio, 11, 16, 17, 19, 29,
31, 32, 93
Coello, Juan, 19, 32
Coello, Pedro, 21
Coliseo, 21, 22
collaborators, 16, 17, 19, 29, 31-32
collective tragedy, 62, 65, 146
comedia, 36, 37, 76, 94, 106, 110,
117, 135, 136, 137
comedia de figurón, 127, 131-132
comedia de magia, 42

Index

Index

Index

Index